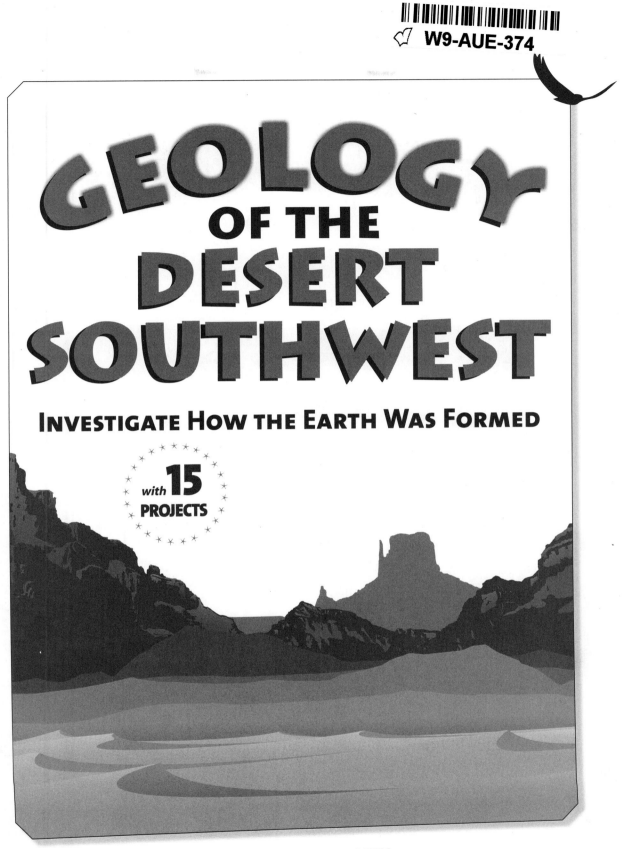

GEOLOGY OF THE DESERT SOUTHWEST

INVESTIGATE HOW THE EARTH WAS FORMED

with **15** PROJECTS

CYNTHIA LIGHT BROWN

Illustrated by Eric Baker

W9-AUE-374

~Titles in the *Build It Yourself* **Series~**

green press
INITIATIVE

Nomad Press is committed to preserving ancient forests and natural resources. We elected to print *Geology of the Desert Southwest: Investigate How the Earth Was Formed* on 4,507 lbs. of Williamsburg Recycled 30 percent offset.

Nomad Press made this paper choice because our printer, Sheridan Books, is a member of Green Press Initiative, a nonprofit program dedicated to supporting authors, publishers, and suppliers in their efforts to reduce their use of fiber obtained from endangered forests. For more information, visit **www.greenpressinitiative.org**

Nomad Press
A division of Nomad Communications
10 9 8 7 6 5 4 3 2 1
Copyright © 2011 by Nomad Press. All rights reserved.
No part of this book may be reproduced in any form without permission in writing from
the publisher, except by a reviewer who may quote brief passages in a review or **for limited educational use**.
The trademark "Nomad Press" and the Nomad Press logo are trademarks of Nomad Communications, Inc.

This book was manufactured by Sheridan Books,
Ann Arbor, MI USA.
August 2011, Job # 328316
ISBN: 978-1-936313-40-2

Illustrations by Eric Baker
Educational Consultant, Marla Conn

Questions regarding the ordering of this book should be addressed to
Independent Publishers Group
814 N. Franklin St.
Chicago, IL 60610
www.ipgbook.com

Nomad Press
2456 Christian St.
White River Junction, VT 05001
www.nomadpress.net

~CONTENTS~

Desert View Watchtower Grand Canyon, Arizona

Arches National Park, Utah

Saguaro National Park, Arizona

GEOLOGY & GEOGRAPHY

The Desert Southwest is a place of searing heat and dry canyons. It's also a land of mountains covered in snow and towering cacti. You can find some of our nation's great landmarks here, like the Grand Canyon and Death Valley.

WORDS TO KNOW

desert: an ecosystem that lacks water, receiving 10 inches or less of precipitation each year. Rain or snow is not evenly distributed throughout the year.

Why does this region hold the great **deserts** of the United States and one of the largest canyons in the world? It has to do with the shape of the land that was formed billions of years ago, and that is still being shaped today.

1

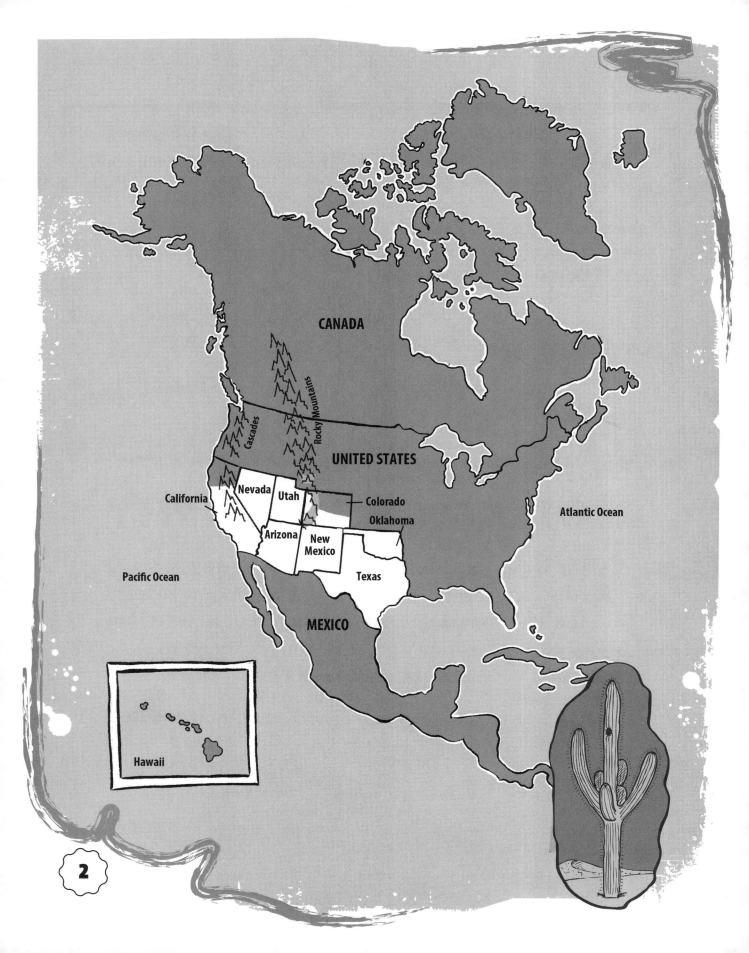

CANADA

UNITED STATES

Cascades

Rocky Mountains

California

Nevada

Utah

Colorado

Arizona

New Mexico

Oklahoma

Texas

Atlantic Ocean

Pacific Ocean

MEXICO

Hawaii

In this book, you'll learn about the great forces that have shaped the mountains, valleys, and plains of the Desert Southwest—how things got where they are, and why. You'll learn about the physical systems, like the weather, rivers, and **ecosystems**. Along the way, you'll collect some interesting facts, such as why the region has the hottest location or the largest salt-water lake in North America. The experiments and projects will help you understand the concepts, like how a salty lake forms.

GEOLOGY: MORE THAN JUST ROCKS

Most people think of **geology** as the study of rocks, but it's much more. When you look at a rock, you can describe its color and shape. But what is even more interesting is how that rock formed, how it got to its present location, and why. That involves seeing the big picture—the picture of the whole earth. Geology is the scientific study of the history and physical nature of the earth. It involves the huge movements of the earth's crust. It also involves the **atmosphere** and **hydrosphere**, because air and water affect the breakdown and formation of rocks.

GEOGRAPHY: MORE THAN JUST STATES AND CAPITALS

When most people think of **geography**, they think of learning the names of capitals and states, or where the largest rivers and mountains are. All of that is important, but geography tells a bigger story. It gives us a big view of the land, and how people interact with the land.

WORDS TO KNOW

ecosystem: a community of plants and animals living in the same area and relying on each other to survive.

geology: the scientific study of the history and physical nature of the earth.

atmosphere: the air surrounding the earth.

hydrosphere: the waters on the earth's surface, including oceans, rivers, lakes, and water vapor in the air.

geography: the study of the earth and its features, especially the shape of the land, and the effect of human activity on the earth.

There are two parts to geography: physical and cultural. Physical geography looks at the features of the earth and atmosphere. It includes mountains, rivers, and **climate**. Physical geography is a lot like geology, but is less about the big forces under the earth's surface, and more about the shape of the land. Cultural geography looks at how people interact with the land, including population, **agriculture**, and recreation. Physical geography and cultural geography are closely tied together. For example, people depend on rivers for water, food, and transportation. But people can also affect rivers by building **dams** or cities on a river.

WORDS TO KNOW

climate: average weather patterns in an area over many years.

agriculture: growing plants and raising animals for food and other products.

dam: a barrier across a river to hold back and control the water.

vegetation: all the plant life in a particular area.

Physical features, like mountains, don't usually follow the exact outlines of states. The southern Rocky Mountains start in northern New Mexico and extend north through Colorado, Wyoming, Idaho, and Montana. When people say the Desert Southwest region, sometimes they mean just the states of New Mexico and Arizona, and sometimes they mean more than that.

This book covers the states of Texas, Oklahoma, Utah, Nevada, New Mexico, and Arizona, as well as southern Colorado, and the southern two-thirds of California. It focuses on the geology and physical geography of the Desert Southwest. Hawaii is mentioned because it is closest to the southwest region.

The Desert Southwest has occupied a unique place in the imagination and culture of America. At first the region seems barren, with little **vegetation** and water. But its wide-open spaces and unique ecosystems reveal a quiet beauty.

4

CHAPTER 1

PLATE TECTONICS

It's no accident that the giant saguaro cactus grows in southern Arizona. Cacti need a dry climate, and southern Arizona receives very little rain. That's no accident either. Much of the rain from the Pacific Ocean is blocked by mountains along the California coast.

WORDS TO KNOW

plate tectonics: the theory that describes how plates move across the earth and interact with each other to produce volcanoes, earthquakes, and mountains.

Why do mountains stretch along the west coast of the United States? **Plate tectonics** is the driving force behind how ALL of the different landscapes formed in the Desert Southwest.

Plate tectonics is the theory that the outer layer of the earth is made up of interconnected plates that are moving around. Together with heat from the sun, the powerful forces inside the earth shape every landscape and ecosystem on the surface of the earth. **Volcanoes**, mountains, valleys, **earthquakes**, and **erosion** all happen where they do because of the movement of the earth's plates. And the locations of the mountains influence weather patterns.

A PEEK INSIDE

The earth may look solid and motionless, but much of it is liquid. It consists of three layers:

The **crust** is the thin, outer layer of the earth. This is the layer that we walk on. It's solid but **brittle**, which means that it breaks when put under pressure.

The **mantle** is the layer below the crust. It is hotter and **denser** here because the temperature and pressure inside the earth increase the deeper you go. The upper mantle is brittle and solid.

The **core** is the center of the earth. It is extremely dense. The inner core is solid because the pressure is so great, while the outer core is liquid. The core is almost as hot as the sun—about 9,000 degrees Fahrenheit (5,000 degrees Celsius).

WORDS TO KNOW

volcano: a vent in the earth's surface through which magma, ash, and gases erupt.

earthquake: a sudden movement in the outer layer of the earth that releases stress built up from the motion of the plates.

erosion: wearing away of rock or soil by water and wind.

crust: the thin, brittle outer layer of the earth. Together with the upper mantle, it forms the lithosphere.

brittle: describes a solid that breaks when put under pressure. A blade of grass will bend, but a dry twig is brittle and will break.

mantle: the middle layer of the earth. The upper mantle, together with the crust, forms the lithosphere.

dense: tightly packed.

core: the center layer of the earth, composed of the metals iron and nickel. The core has two parts—a solid inner core and a liquid outer core.

Together, the crust and the upper mantle form the **lithosphere**, the hard outer layer of the earth. The lithosphere is broken into plates. Below the plates is a layer called the **asthenosphere**. It is partially **molten** and can flow slowly without breaking—a bit like Silly Putty.

THE EARTH'S PUZZLE

The hard outer layer of the earth, the lithosphere, is broken up into about 12 large sections, called plates. There are also several smaller plates. The plates fit together like a jigsaw puzzle. Most are part **oceanic** and part **continental**. For example, the North American Plate includes nearly all of North America and the western half of the Atlantic Ocean.

WORDS TO KNOW

lithosphere: the rigid outer layer of the earth that includes the crust and the upper mantle.

asthenosphere: the semi-molten middle layer of the earth that includes the lower mantle. Much of the asthenosphere flows slowly, like Silly Putty.

molten: melted by heat to form a liquid.

oceanic: in or from the ocean.

continental: relating to the earth's continents.

current: a constantly moving mass of liquid.

Did You Know?

You might have heard of the earth's plates being sections of the earth's crust. That's partly correct. The tectonic plates are made of the crust and the upper mantle, which together are called the lithosphere. But most people just call it the crust because it's easier to remember.

The plates are in constant slow motion! That's because the layer just under the plates—the asthenosphere—is very hot. The heat causes the molten rocks there to move around in huge, rotating **currents** called convection cells. These convection cells move the plates above, which are floating like rafts on the hot goo below. The plates also help themselves move along. The older part of a plate is colder and denser. When it sinks into the mantle it pulls the rest of the plate with it and keeps the cycle going. Plates move between 1 and 6 inches per year (2–15 centimeters).

WORDS TO KNOW

divergent boundary: where two plates are moving in opposite directions, sometimes called a rift zone. New crust forms from magma pushing through the crust here.

magma: partially melted rock below the surface of the earth.

rifting: when the lithosphere splits apart.

convergent boundary: where two plates come together, forming mountains and volcanoes, and causing earthquakes.

subduction: when one plate slides underneath another plate.

ON THE EDGE

Volcanoes and earthquakes don't just happen. They're arranged in patterns. You'll find lots of volcanoes around the rim of the Pacific Ocean, but none in Kansas. That's because most of the action happens where one plate meets another. This is called a plate boundary. There are three different kinds of plate boundaries:

Divergent boundaries are where two plates move apart from each other. They do this because the hot molten goo beneath, called **magma**, is pushing upward. This causes **rifting**. The hot goo pushes out and solidifies to form new rocks. Nearly all of the earth's new crust forms at divergent boundaries. The Desert Southwest has two areas of rifting.

Convergent boundaries are where two plates collide. What happens depends on whether the plates are oceanic or continental. One type of collision is when an oceanic plate collides with a continental plate. Because the oceanic plate is denser and thinner than the continental plate, it slides underneath the continental plate. This is called **subduction**.

As the subducted oceanic plate sinks lower, its weight pulls the rest of the plate along as well. The sinking plate encounters a lot of heat and pressure. This causes the plate to release hot gas and steam, which rises and melts the rock above. The melted rock, the magma, also rises to the surface, creating volcanoes. In the Pacific Northwest, this is happening right now to create the Cascade Mountains with explosive volcanoes like Mount St. Helens.

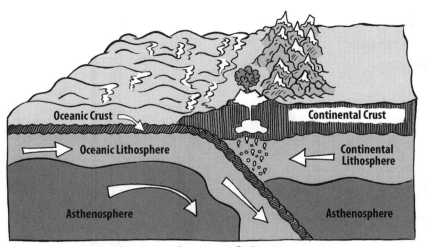

Oceanic Crust · Continental Crust · Oceanic Lithosphere · Continental Lithosphere · Asthenosphere · Asthenosphere

Oceanic Continental Convergance

WORDS TO KNOW

transform boundary: where two plates slide against each other.

fault: a crack in the outer layer of the earth.

hotspot: a small area where hot magma rises, usually in the middle of a plate.

If a continental plate collides with another continental plate, they both buckle upwards, forming mountains. That's what is happening now where the Indian Plate and the Eurasian Plate are colliding. The result is the Himalaya Mountains, which include Mt. Everest, the highest mountain in the world. Long ago, the Brooks Range in northern Alaska formed when continental crust slammed into North America.

Transform boundaries are where two plates grind against each other as they move side by side in opposite directions. As the plates move past each other they sometimes suddenly slip. This creates a big lurch, or earthquake. The famous San Andreas **Fault** in California is part of a transform boundary between the North American and Pacific Plates. This is why California has so many earthquakes. A transform boundary also runs through Denali National Park in Alaska.

Hotspots are areas of strong activity, but they aren't on the edge of plates. These small, extremely hot regions usually occur in the middle of a plate. They exist because hot material, probably from deep in the mantle, makes its way to the surface. The Hawaiian Islands formed when the Pacific Plate slowly made its way over a hotspot.

Hawaii is a classic example of the hotspot theory of plate tectonics.

While Hawaii is quite far from any plate boundaries, it has very active volcanoes that have formed from magma. As the Pacific Plate moves over the hotspot, the magma produces volcanoes. The Hawaiian islands have about 125 volcanoes that stretch 3,600 miles (5,800 kilometers). There's also a hotspot under Yellowstone National Park, but parts of Oregon and Montana have moved over this hotspot in the past.

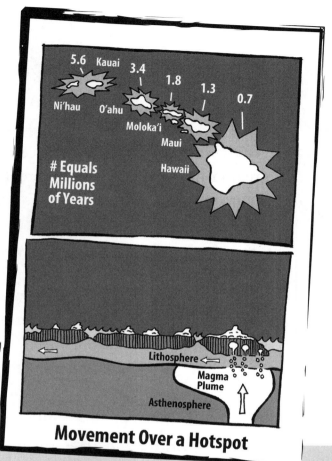

Movement Over a Hotspot

GIANT CONVEYOR BELT

The movement of the plates acts a bit like a giant, wide, conveyor belt. This conveyor belt is like a flat escalator, used to move people or things across a long space. At divergent boundaries, magma pushes through, cools, and forms new crust.

The lithosphere is like a rigid board, though, and as two plates move apart, the other end of each plate collides with another lithosphere. At the collision, one plate is subducted, or pushed under, and melts. So lithosphere is created on one end, and destroyed on another. Just like conveyor belts, or the stairs on an escalator, lithosphere appears on one end and disappears on the other end.

TECTONIC HISTORY OF THE DESERT SOUTHWEST

The Desert Southwest has a varied **tectonic** history. Most places in the region have experienced different things happening at different points in time. At one point, an area might have been a valley or low-lying area with rivers running through it and **sediments** piling up. Much later, that area might have been pushed up into mountains.

WORDS TO KNOW

tectonic: relating to the forces that produce movement and changes in the earth's crust.

sediment: loose rock particles such as sand or clay.

geologist: a scientist who studies the earth and its movements.

craton: the stable, central part of a continent.

accretion: the process of crust being added to a craton.

The rocks often record this history, but it can be hard to sort out what happened when. Sometimes rocks have been completely removed due to erosion or subduction. As you might guess, the farther back in time you go, the harder it is to tell what happened. But **geologists** have pieced together a rough picture of the tectonic past.

The ancient continent of North America has, at times, been joined with other continents into large supercontinents, and at other times separated by itself. The central part of the continent, called the **craton**, is the oldest part. It formed billions of years ago.

The North American craton grew as pieces of smaller continents and island arcs slammed onto the edges of the continent. At the same time, there was lots of magma rising and cooling in the new blocks of crust. This process is called **accretion**.

In the Desert Southwest, accretion happened from about 2 billion years ago until about 1 billion years ago. The areas that were added include most of Utah, Arizona, New Mexico, and northern Texas.

For a long time, things were relatively quiet for the region. At different times, shallow seas covered much of the interior of North America, including the Southwest. Lots of sediments settled on top of the older rocks in the craton.

Then things changed. A supercontinent that contained all the land on Earth slowly formed about 300 million years ago. It is called **Pangaea**. After about 100 million years, Pangaea started to break apart. This affected the east and west of the Desert Southwest quite differently.

WORDS TO KNOW

Pangaea: a huge supercontinent that existed about 300 million years ago. It contained all the land on Earth.

Pangaea is a Greek word that means "all lands."

On the eastern end of what is now the Desert Southwest, the Atlantic Ocean opened up as rifting began there. New oceanic crust formed from the rifting and attached to continental crust to form the North American Plate. But the ocean and continent move together here—the oceanic crust doesn't subduct beneath the continental crust. Eastern Texas was formed at this stage with sediments flowing onto its platform.

At the western end, the oceanic plate called Farallon was subducting beneath the North American Plate. This subduction continued for a long time, and is still occurring off the coast of Oregon and Washington. Around 70 million years ago the subducting oceanic crust flattened out somewhat and caused the crust to buckle inside the North American continent, creating the Rocky Mountains that extend south into New Mexico. This also caused the crust around Texas and Oklahoma to become much thicker.

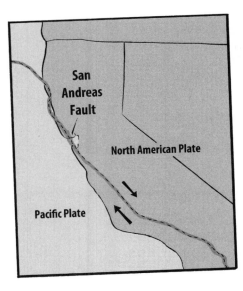

San Andreas Fault

North American Plate

Pacific Plate

Then about 28 million years ago, the subduction off the West Coast changed. The Farallon Plate had been subducting under the entire west coast of North America. Then the spreading center of the Pacific Plate reached the subduction zone along California. From California and farther south, the Farallon Plate was completely consumed. At this point, the Pacific Plate began to break off pieces of North America and the San Andreas Fault System developed. The San Andreas is a right lateral system of faults. This means that the right side of the fault is moving southeast and the left side is moving northwest.

The North American continent has moved about 282 miles southeast with respect to the Pacific Plate.

Because the Pacific Plate was pulling the edge of North America northwest, North America stretched, particularly around the state of Nevada. As the stretching occurred, the crust thinned and cracked as it pulled apart. This created large faults that run roughly north to south.

Did You Know?

Most of the ancient North America craton is now covered in sediments, but in places the old rocks peek through. The bottoms of canyons, like the Grand Canyon, have rocks that tell the tectonic story from that ancient time.

WORDS TO KNOW

plateau: a relatively level, or flat area.

elevation: a measurement of height above sea level.

Colorado Plateau: a large, roughly circular area of land, high in elevation.

One area that has remained relatively untouched is a **plateau** high in **elevation** in Colorado. The **Colorado Plateau** is an area covering northeast Arizona, southeast Utah, southwest Colorado, and northwest New Mexico.

WHAT'S HAPPENING NOW?

There are four different kinds of things happening tectonically in the Southwest. Moving from east to west, they are:

Stable tectonics, receiving sedimentation—The area including Texas, Oklahoma, and eastern New Mexico is a stable tectonic area. There is no subduction occurring between the oceanic crust and the continental crust because they are slowly but quietly moving west together. The area is low-lying and receives sediments flowing from the Rocky Mountains in the west, and the Appalachians in the east. In places, sediments are up to 40,000 feet thick (12,000 meters)!

Rifting—There are two areas where the North American Plate is stretching apart. The Rio Grande Rift is a smaller area extending like a finger into New Mexico and southern Colorado. The Basin and Range Province is a larger area covering southern Arizona and California, all of Nevada, and small parts of Oregon, Utah, and Idaho. These two areas join together in the south and look on a map a bit like a large ladle. The rifting is occurring because the western edge of North America is being pulled farther west and north by the motion of the Pacific Plate, stretching the continent apart.

If the stretching continues, an ocean could open here millions of years from now.

High, dry and stable—If the Basin and Range forms a ladle-like shape, the Colorado Plateau is what's inside the ladle. It is a roughly circular-shaped island of tectonic stability surrounded by the Basin and Range and Rocky Mountains. Since it sits high in elevation, it is not receiving sediments like the low-lying areas in Texas and Oklahoma. Instead, it is being carved by rivers cutting down through its layers. It's no accident that the Grand Canyon is located in the Colorado Plateau!

14

PLATE TECTONICS: THE ORIGINAL RECYCLER

The earth has been recycling materials for over 4 billion years! Every rock that you see has come from another kind of rock. And every rock that you see will eventually become another one. All this recycling happens because of the movement of the plates pushing everything around. To understand this recycling, you have to know a bit about the three main types of rocks.

Igneous Rocks form when molten rock cools. As you go deeper beneath the surface of the earth, it becomes hotter. At around 25 miles beneath the surface (40 kilometers), it's hot enough to melt rocks. When that magma comes to the surface, it cools into igneous rocks.

Sedimentary Rocks form when small particles of rock, called sediments, are pressed tightly together into rock. Sediments come from other rocks being eroded, or broken into smaller pieces by wind, water, ice, and gravity. Sedimentary rocks can also form from the remains of plants or animals being pressed together. When seawater evaporates, the minerals and salts in the water stay behind and can form into rock.

Metamorphic Rocks form when heat or pressure changes rocks into new rocks. Pressure, like temperature, increases as you go farther beneath the surface of the earth. If rocks are pushed under the surface, but not far enough to melt, they can be changed into new rocks without first melting. Igneous rocks can be eroded into sediments, which then form sedimentary rocks. Those sedimentary rocks can then be buried and heated and squeezed to form metamorphic rocks. Metamorphic rocks can be pushed down into the mantle and melted, to later form igneous rocks. Or it could happen in reverse, because any type of rock can form from any type of rock.

Transform fault—Western California sits on the San Andreas Fault System. Here, the Pacific and North American Plates grind against each other in a zone of transform faults. The Pacific Plate is moving northwest, while the North American Plate is moving southeast. This plate boundary is quite active, with many earthquakes!

MAKE YOUR OWN
SWEET PLATE BOUNDARIES

SUPPLIES

- candy bar with layers such as a Milky Way
- solid chocolate candy bar
- table knife (one that isn't sharp)

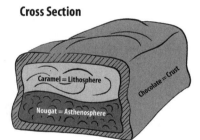

Cross Section

Caramel = Lithosphere

Chocolate = Crust

Nougat = Asthenosphere

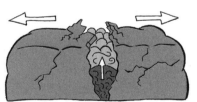

Divergent Plate Boundary

1 Cut one end from the layered candy bar—just enough to see inside. This is called the cross-section of the candy bar. How is the candy bar like the earth? How are the layers like the layers in the earth? How are they different?

2 Using the knife, make two or three cracks in the chocolate across the top middle part of the layered candy bar. The chocolate on each side of the cracks represents different plates in the lithosphere. Grab the candy bar on each end and slowly pull it apart, about 1 inch or less (2½ centimeters). What does the gooey layer underneath do? This represents the asthenosphere, which is soft and stretches. The pulling apart represents a divergent plate boundary. During real rifting, though, the asthenosphere (gooey layer) would well up with magma erupting at the surface.

3 Push the layers back together, then push one side forward and pull the other side back. Do you feel resistance? This represents a transform plate boundary.

Transform Plate Boundary

4 Take half the layered candy bar in one hand, and the solid chocolate bar in the other hand. Push the two candy bars together, letting the solid chocolate bar go underneath the layered bar. This represents a convergent boundary. The solid chocolate bar is oceanic lithosphere, which is thinner and denser, and the layered bar is continental lithosphere. The oceanic lithosphere subducts beneath the continental lithosphere.

What's Happening?

The earth is composed of layers. A Milky Way has an outside top chocolate layer and a caramel layer below that is like the earth's lithosphere. The fluffy nougat layer underneath is like the asthenosphere.

MAKE YOUR OWN
RIFT ZONE

1 Place the tables close together so they are almost touching. Place the chairs on the outside with the chair backs towards the tables.

2 With a friend, make two extra-long pieces of paper by taping papers together end-to-end. Each paper should be longer than the width of the table.

3 Kneel on the chairs on opposite sides of the table, facing each other. Each of you should take one piece of long paper in both hands and lower it through the space between the table, while still holding onto the paper. Your hands should almost touch.

4 Now both at the same time, slowly pull your papers up through the opening and onto your table towards yourself. Try to pull at the same speed. When your hands reach the side of the table closest to you, pull the paper down so that it drapes off the side into the space between your chair and the table.

SUPPLIES

- a friend
- 2 or more small tables, the same height
- 2 chairs
- several pieces of paper
- tape
- colored markers

5 Do it again, but this time stop pulling after a few seconds and have a friend color a stripe on each paper where it is coming up through the opening, parallel to the opening. Pull again for a few seconds, then have your friend color another stripe on each paper in a different color, but either wider or narrower than the first. Keep doing this until both papers are filled with stripes.

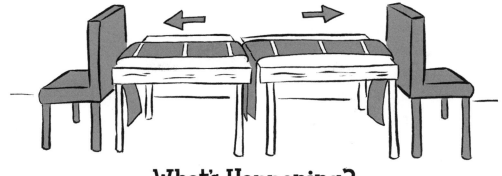

What's Happening?

The opening between the tables is like a divergent plate boundary. As the papers (plates) pull apart, more paper (magma) comes up from the mantle below. This is the magma that cools into oceanic crust. On the other end of each table, the plate subducts under another plate (the chairs).

Earth is like a giant magnet with its magnetic poles close to the North and South Poles. Geologists have discovered that the magnetic field of the earth can reverse itself—the magnetic North Pole becomes the magnetic South Pole and vice versa. This changes the way a compass points. These reversals can happen every few thousand or millions of years.

The stripes you drew on the papers represent oceanic rocks that contain iron. As magma cools, the iron in it lines up with the magnetic North and South Poles. When the rock spreads out from the ridge, the iron doesn't change direction. When there is a magnetic reversal, the iron in new oceanic rocks lines up in the opposite direction. As the oceanic crust moves away from the spreading ridge, it has magnetic stripes parallel to the ridge—just like your papers.

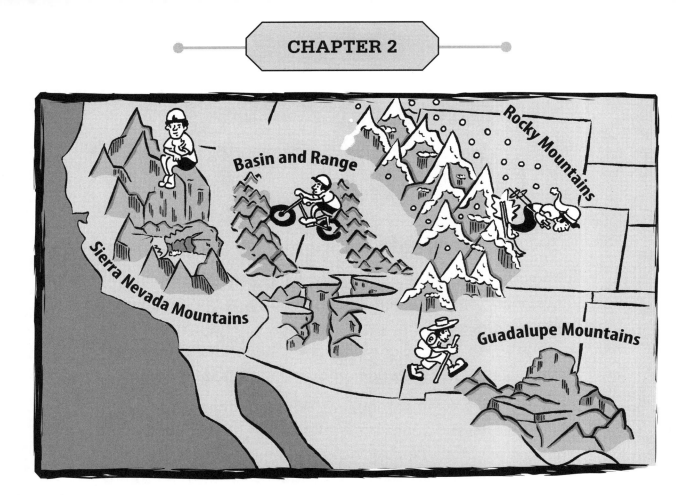

CHAPTER 2

MOUNTAINS

The Desert Southwest region has a wide variety of mountains that formed in different ways. These include the southern Rocky Mountains in New Mexico, the Guadalupe Mountains of Texas and New Mexico, the mountains formed in the deserts of Nevada, and the ladle of the Basin and Range Mountains. Even in the desert, mountains can rise so high that they are capped in snow, creating a stunning sight.

SOUTHERN ROCKY MOUNTAINS

The Rocky Mountains, also called the Rockies, are a major mountain chain that runs from New Mexico to Canada. The southern Rockies in New Mexico include the Sangre de Cristo Mountains, the Tusas Mountains, and the Sierra Nacimiento.

WORDS TO KNOW

organism: any living thing.

altitude: the height above the level of the sea.

The rocks at the core of these mountains formed when the North American continent was being put together. This was between 1.6 and 1.7 billion years ago, a time when the only life that existed was single-celled **organisms**. Much later, these rocks were pushed up during mountain-forming events. Finally, the land started pulling apart, creating the Rio Grande Rift that separated these mountains.

SIERRA NEVADA

The Sierra Nevada Mountains run north to south for about 400 miles along the eastern side of California (644 kilometers). These high, majestic mountains have served as inspiration for many, as well as an obstacle to travel.

Did You Know?

The Sierra Nevada Mountains are home to the largest mountain lake in North America, Lake Tahoe. The lake sits at an **altitude** of 6,225 feet (1,897 meters), and is 191 square miles in area (495 square kilometers). There are 16 countries in the world that have a smaller land area than Lake Tahoe.

While the Sierra Nevada look like they're joined with the Cascades to the north in Oregon and Washington, they formed in different ways and are much older. The Sierra Nevada formed millions of years ago around the time when dinosaurs lived. Over and over, magma erupted into volcanoes in this area. Beneath the volcanoes, more magma cooled into rocks before reaching the surface, forming granite.

Over time, the volcanic rocks eroded away, exposing the granite underneath. The granite mountains weren't very high, but when the Basin and Range region to the east starting stretching apart and tilting, it lifted up the Sierra Nevada along its east side. Imagine the granite rocks being like a wooden block that you're looking at from the side. If you placed a few pennies underneath the right (east) side of the block, the block would have a steep slope on the east side, and a gentle slope on the west side. That's just what happened with the Sierra Nevada. And it's still being lifted up!

BASIN AND RANGE

The Basin and Range is unique in the United States. It is a series of north-south mountains (ranges) and flat valley floors (basins) that alternate back and forth—a long mountain chain, then a long valley, and so on. On a map, the area is shaped a bit like a ladle. It covers all of the state of Nevada and bits of Idaho, Oregon, and Utah, scooping down through California and Arizona, then up again into New Mexico. It also extends south into Mexico.

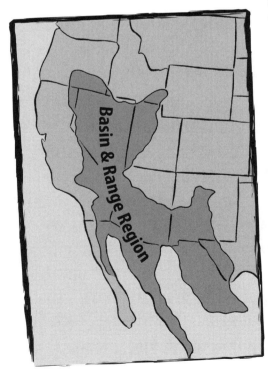

The Basin and Range began forming about 20 million years ago when the lithosphere started stretching apart in this region—and it's still stretching!

It's stretching because of the way the tectonic plates are shifting at the San Andreas Fault. As the continental lithosphere pulls apart, the lithosphere in this area stretches and becomes thinner. This causes a few things to happen.

• Because the lithosphere is brittle, when it's pulled apart, it doesn't stretch like gooey taffy. Instead, it breaks apart along faults into huge blocks of rocks miles wide and thousands of feet thick. These blocks of rocks tilted as they were pulled apart, so on one side of the fault the rocks moved down compared to rocks on the other side of the fault. The Basin and Range region has about 400 mountain blocks that have tilted like this.

Did You Know?

Geologists predict the lithosphere will keep pulling apart in the Basin and Range— eventually rifting into two pieces with a shallow ocean filling in.

• As rifting begins, the hot asthenosphere underneath moves closer to the surface, pushing the entire region higher in elevation. The asthenosphere also pushes through the crust as volcanoes.

• As rifting continues and the crust thins out, it starts to sink back down in elevation. So the longer ago rifting began, the lower in elevation the area. Rifting began earlier in the southern part of the region, so it's lower in elevation—like Death Valley National Park, which you'll learn more about in Chapter 4.

Usually, we think of rocks that are higher in elevation as being younger. Sediments are deposited with the oldest layers on the bottom. But in the Basin and Range, the mountains are generally older than the basins between. That's because during rifting, the valleys actually dropped down with respect to the mountains. So mountaintops typically have old rocks that formed hundreds of millions of years ago, while the valleys have much younger rocks.

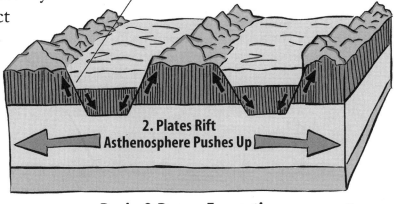

1. Lithosphere Breaks Along Fault Lines

2. Plates Rift Asthenosphere Pushes Up

Basin & Range Formation

23

YOSEMITE NATIONAL PARK

WORDS TO KNOW

glacier: a huge mass of ice and snow.

Yosemite National Park has some of the most amazing landscapes in America—huge cliffs, waterfalls, polished rocks, and gigantic granite domes. John Muir, a famous naturalist, once said of Yosemite, "It is by far the grandest of all the special temples of Nature I was ever permitted to enter."

Like the rest of the Sierra Nevada, most of Yosemite is composed of granite rocks. The granite formed from magma cooling beneath the surface of the earth. It was later lifted up and exposed when the rocks above eroded away. Granite doesn't have layers and it's very durable, so it can form large blocks and domes.

Much of Yosemite's beauty is due to **glaciers**. A glacier forms when more snow falls in the winter than melts in the summer. The earth periodically goes through warming and cooling periods. During colder periods, glaciers formed in the high mountains of the Sierra Nevada, including at Yosemite. Why do geologists think glaciers carved this landscape? Yosemite Valley offers some clues that tell us a glacier has been around.

Did You Know?

The tallest waterfall in North America is Yosemite Falls in Yosemite National Park, which is 2,425 feet high (739 meters).

U-Shaped Valley: River valleys are V-shaped, from the river slowly cutting into the rock. Glaciers follow the path of rivers because, like rivers, they are seeking the fastest way downhill. But glaciers are wider, and the rocks they carry carve out a valley with a "U" shape. Even though they are slow, glaciers are extremely powerful. They move aside just about anything in their way—trees, rocks, and even large boulders. Glaciers become a bit like sandpaper as they pluck up rocks and carry them downhill. This sandpaper erodes the land into U-shaped valleys and sharp mountain peaks. Yosemite Valley in the park is a flat-floored valley floor about 7 miles long and 1 mile wide with a classic U shape (11 kilometers long and 1.6 kilometers wide).

Hanging Valley: When a smaller glacier in a side canyon feeds into a larger glacier, the smaller glacier doesn't cut as deeply as the larger glacier. After they melt, the smaller glaciers leave behind smaller valleys high up on the mountainsides that look like they're hanging. Yosemite Valley was carved by a large glacier. Many smaller glaciers flowed into this large one from the side valleys. Then when the glaciers melted, the smaller side streams were much higher in elevation. These are called "hanging valleys."

Polished Rock: As the glacier drags smaller rocks over bedrock below, the smaller rocks grind a smooth or grooved surface.

Cirques: These are large bowls that form at the top, or head, of a glacier. Often the bowl fills with water, forming a small lake.

Moraines: When a glacier melts, the rocks it picked up are dumped out. Because the glacier acts like a conveyor belt made out of ice, more and more rocks are dumped out, forming a pile of rocks at the bottom and sides of the glacier. Recent moraines look like just that—a pile of rocks. Older moraines are covered by soil and plants. Moraines can be found in Yosemite Valley and other locations in the Park.

WORDS TO KNOW

reef: a ridge of coral or rock close to the surface of a body of water.

GUADALUPE MOUNTAINS

The Guadalupe Mountains stretch from western Texas into southeastern New Mexico. They contain the highest point in Texas.

About 265 million years ago, a vast warm sea covered the area. A **reef** formed about 400 miles long (640 kilometers). Later, the reef was lifted up by tectonic forces to form the mountains. It's one of the best-preserved fossilized reefs in the world. At the tops of the Guadalupe Mountains, you can find fossils of sea creatures such as algae, sponges, clams, and sea urchins—over 8,000 feet above sea level (2,400 meters)!

HIGHEST SOUTHWEST MOUNTAINS

- Mt. Whitney, 14,494 feet *(4,418 meters)*
- Boundary Peak, 13,140 feet *(4,005 meters)*
- Kings Peak, 13,528 feet *(4,123 meters)*
- Humphreys Peak, 12,633 feet *(3,851 meters)*
- Wheeler Peak, 13,161 feet *(4,011 meters)*
- Black Mesa, 4,973 feet *(1,516 meters)*
- Guadalupe Peak, 8,749 feet *(2,667 meters)*

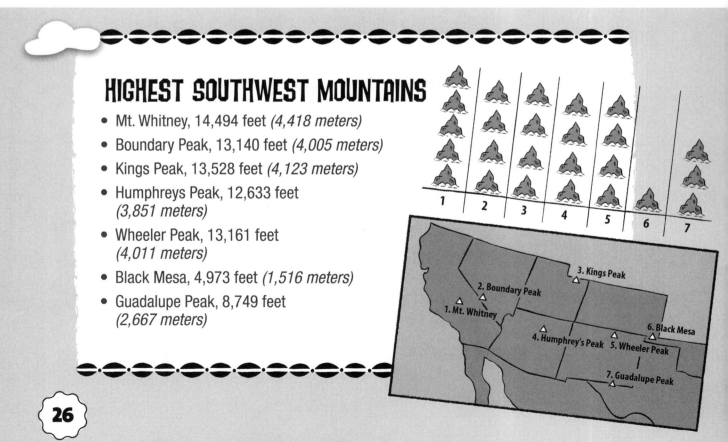

MAKE YOUR OWN
BASIN AND RANGE

1 Place the books upright next to each other, between the two bookends. Their bindings should face up.

2 Slowly pull apart the bookends. Let the books tilt to one side as you pull, until the books are at a 30-to-45-degree angle.

SUPPLIES

- 6 hardback books about the same size
- 2 bookends

What's Happening

The faults are the boundaries between the books. Faults are cracks in the earth where rocks move relative to each other. When the earth's crust was stretched in an east-west direction, it caused the surface rocks to break into huge blocks that tilted like row of books on a shelf.

CHAPTER 3

VOLCANOES AND EARTHQUAKES

Have you ever heard the phrase "rock-solid?" It seems like nothing could be more solid and reassuring than the earth beneath our feet. But deep beneath the surface, the earth is in turmoil. The rocks aren't always solid. We aren't usually aware of that turmoil, but sometimes volcanoes spew molten lava. Sometimes earthquakes shake the earth.

The Desert Southwest has both volcanoes and earthquakes, from volcanoes in New Mexico to active earthquakes in California.

VOLCANOES!

Volcanoes are formed when magma comes to the surface. Sometimes the liquid rock cools before it reaches the surface. When that happens, it forms rocks such as granite. But when the magma comes all the way to the surface before it cools, it's called lava, and it comes out through an opening in the earth called a volcano.

WORDS TO KNOW

viscous: how easily a substance flows. Honey is very viscous, while water is not viscous.

silica: a mineral existing in over one-quarter of the earth's crust.

basalt: a volcanic rock that is dark gray and fine-grained.

Lava can slowly bubble out of the earth or it can shoot out violently. What's the formula for an explosive volcano? Thick lava with lots of water vapor.

Liquids that are very **viscous**, like honey, resist flow. Less viscous liquids, like water, flow easily. Lava that has lots of **silica** is lighter colored, more viscous, and likely to explode. Darker lavas with less silica (that form rocks such as **basalt**) are less viscous and more likely to flow smoothly.

It also depends on how much gas, mainly water vapor, is still in the lava when it reaches the surface. Lots of dissolved gas creates pressure in the lava. This makes it more explosive, like a soda can that's been shaken. Gas is trapped more easily in more viscous lava.

29

BASALT

Basalt is an igneous rock that forms when certain types of lava flows onto the surface of the earth. It's dark gray to black and very fine-grained, which means the mineral grains are too small to be seen. Basalt is quite dense, or heavy, because its minerals are dense. It's the most common type of rock on Earth, but most basalt is located on the ocean's floors.

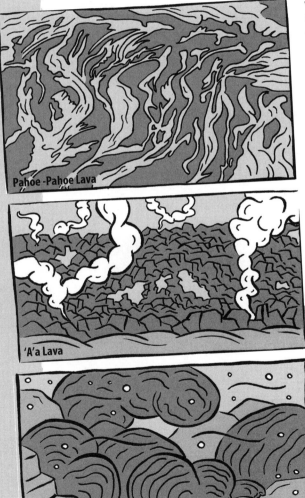

Pahoe-Pahoe Lava

'A'a Lava

Pillow Lava

Sometimes basalt lava flows from a central vent, or opening, and forms a cone—what we call a volcano. But basalt lava can also flow out quietly from long openings in the earth, called fissures.

You can tell something about where and how basalt lava erupted by what the basalt rocks look like.

• Pahoe-pahoe has a ropy, smooth surface. This type of basalt lava is not very viscous, which means that it flows easily. Pahoe-pahoe is a Hawaiian term that means "smooth, unbroken lava."

• 'A'a is more viscous than pahoe-pahoe. It has a rough, jagged surface with broken blocks of lava. Sometimes lava that forms pahoe-pahoe basalt later forms 'a'a basalt as it travels farther from the point of eruption and has time to cool somewhat. 'A'a is a Hawaiian term that means "rough lava" or "burn."

• Pillow basalt comes from basalt lava that erupts underwater. The surface cools very fast from the seawater. This makes the lava form a pillow shape.

TYPES OF VOLCANOES

There are four main types of volcanoes.

• **Shield volcanoes** are large but low, resembling a warrior's shield lying on the ground. These volcanoes erupt quietly. They slowly eject a fluid lava that can flow a long way before it cools. Examples of shield volcanoes are the volcanoes of Hawaii.

WORDS TO KNOW

shield volcano: a volcano formed from the flow of runny, non-explosive lava.

stratovolcano: a classic, cone-shaped volcano with alternating layers of runny lava flows and more explosive volcanic deposits.

Cross Section of
Shield Volcano

Cross Section of
Stratovolcano

• **Stratovolcanoes** are also called composite volcanoes. They have a classic, cone shape and can erupt explosively. Sometimes stratovolcanoes blow off their tops. They also produce pyroclastic flows, which are deadly avalanches of extremely hot gases, ash, and rocks. Stratovolcanoes include Mt. Taylor in northwest New Mexico and Mt. Shasta in northern California.

WORDS TO KNOW

cinder cone: a small, steep-sided volcano, built by ash and small cinders.

volcanic dome: a volcano formed by thick lava oozing out. The lava is too thick to travel far and builds up into a dome.

• **Cinder cones** are small, steep-sided hills that have a classic, volcano shape. They are built by cinders that were ejected and cooled while gliding through the air. When they erupt, cinder cones look like a lava fountain. Examples of cinder cones are the Bandera Crater and a chain of cinder cones near Grants, New Mexico, as well as Sunset Crater near Flagstaff, Arizona.

• **Volcanic domes** happen when lava that is too thick to flow oozes out of a volcano. It slowly builds up into a volcanic dome. It's a bit like toothpaste where the cap is left off and the toothpaste dries out. That might sound slow and boring, but the pressure can build up and make these volcanoes very explosive. Volcanic domes can be found at Lassen Volcano National Park in California.

Cross Section of Cinder Cone Volcano

Cross Section of Lava Dome Volcano

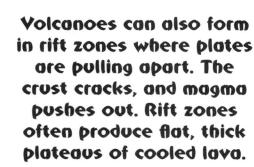

Volcanoes can also form in rift zones where plates are pulling apart. The crust cracks, and magma pushes out. Rift zones often produce flat, thick plateaus of cooled lava.

HAWAII

Hawaii is one big series of volcanoes. In fact, the entire state is made of basalt, formed over many years. Its lava is young—a mere 1 million years old! The magma chamber is ½ to 3 miles below (1 to 5 kilometers).

The islands of Hawaii are prime examples of hotspot activity. Hotspots are small, extremely hot regions beneath the surface of the earth that usually occur in the middle of a plate. As material rises over a hotspot, it melts.

When a plate moves over a hotspot that's under the ocean, large amounts of lava erupt, building broad shield volcanoes on the ocean floor. These volcanoes grow larger and higher as more lava erupts, until finally the volcano breaks through the surface of the water and forms an island. If you look at the map of Hawaii, you can see that the volcanoes are trailing in a curved line. As a volcano moves past the hotspot, that volcano slowly dies out and a new one forms over the hotspot. The older, extinct volcanoes are lower due to erosion and because the entire crust in the area cools and sinks. So volcanoes farthest from the hotspot are the lowest in elevation and are the smallest islands.

The Pacific Plate is moving northwest about 4 inches per year over the Hawaiian hotspot (10 centimeters), so the youngest, tallest volcanic islands are in the southeast.

When a volcano is over the hotspot, it erupts continuously. This is happening now on the island of Hawaii, which has five major volcanoes. It can spew out as much as a cubic mile of lava every 100 years (1½ cubic kilometers). Eruptions typically start at the summit and can travel long distances. In 1984, an eruption on Mauna Loa lasted three weeks and lava traveled miles away. A huge amount of basalt has formed from these volcanoes over time. In fact, the amount of basalt in the island of Hawaii is as much as the volume of rocks in the entire Sierra Nevada mountain range. Most of Hawaii's basalt is underwater.

Did You Know?

If you visit Hawaii Volcanoes National Park, you can see ash venting out of the summit of Kilauea Volcano. The park has two of the world's most active volcanoes: Kilauea and Mauna Loa.

Kauai
Ni'hau
O'ahu
Moloka'i
Lanai
Maui
Hawaii

VALLES CALDERA—SUPERVOLCANO!

You may have heard of the eruption of Mount St. Helens in 1980 in Washington State. It killed 57 people and destroyed bridges, railways, trees, and 200 homes. But compared with eruptions from a volcano in northeast New Mexico, called the Valles Caldera, it was a baby.

WORDS TO KNOW

caldera: a bowl-like depression at the top of a volcano. It forms when the magma chamber underneath is emptied and collapses.

dormant: to be in a resting and inactive state.

The Valles Caldera is a supervolcano that is capable of producing thousands of times as much ash and lava as most volcanoes. The rim of the **caldera** is 12 miles in diameter (19 kilometers) and is the only volcanic caldera in the world to have a paved road inside it.

The caldera formed during eruptions that occurred between 1.6 and 1.2 million years ago. Each one of the explosive eruptions was at least 250 times as large as the Mount St. Helens eruption. Because there was so much magma, the magma chamber collapsed afterward and formed the huge Valles Caldera. There have been much smaller eruptions since then. Luckily for us, the last eruption was about 50,000 years ago.

Did You Know?

An active volcano is a volcano that has erupted in recorded history. Geologists think it will erupt again, probably in the next 200 years. A **dormant** volcano is a "sleepy" volcano that hasn't erupted in recorded history, but could erupt again. An extinct volcano is one that hasn't erupted in many thousands of years, and isn't expected to erupt again.

TRY THIS!

Ask an adult for permission to try this experiment. Get two cans of soda. Open one and let it sit for a few hours. Now go outside, shake the second can of soda, and open it. Make sure that you point the opening of the can away from you when you open it. What happens? Now taste the soda that's been sitting out and the soda you just opened. Can you feel the difference in the fizziness?

Soda has dissolved gas in it, just like lava. When the gas has lots of time to escape, the soda goes flat. The same thing happens to lava that loses its gas as it rises to the surface. It goes flat and just pours out onto the surface without much fizz. But if there's plenty of gas still trapped in your soda, or in the lava, then look out!

EARTHQUAKES!

When stress builds up in rocks, they can suddenly lurch into a new position. That lurching is called an earthquake. Most earthquakes happen along faults, which are cracks in the lithosphere, and especially at plate boundaries.

When an earthquake occurs, it releases huge amounts of energy. Waves of energy travel out in all directions as **seismic waves**. It's a bit like tossing a large rock into a pond. The ripples of water spread out in all directions.

WORDS TO KNOW

seismic waves: waves of energy generated from earthquakes that travel through the earth.

seismograph: an instrument that measures vibrations under the ground.

Did You Know?

Each year there are about 500,000 earthquakes that are detectable by **seismographs**. About 100,000 of them can be felt by humans. About 100 of them cause damage. In southern California alone, there are about 10,000 detectable earthquakes each year.

SEISMIC WAVES

There are different types of seismic waves, and they travel at different rates.

P waves, or pressure waves are the fastest waves. They can reach the other side of the earth in 20 minutes. Pressure waves vibrate the rocks in a push and pull movement in the same direction that the waves travel. They are like a hammer pounding on rock.

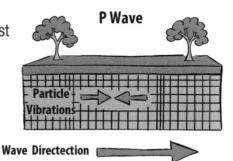

S waves, or shear waves (also called secondary waves) move the rocks back and forth perpendicular to the direction the waves travel. S waves travel at about half the speed of P waves. But when they reach the surface, look out! They can shake buildings back and forth.

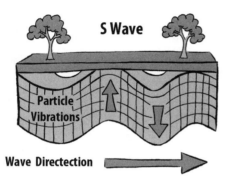

Surface waves are the most destructive earthquake waves. These long, slow waves happen when the energy reaches the surface of the earth. One type of surface wave is called a love wave, which shakes the earth from side to side. The other type of surface wave is the Rayleigh wave. It's a rolling wave: people standing on the surface feel like they're standing on a ship rolling on big ocean waves.

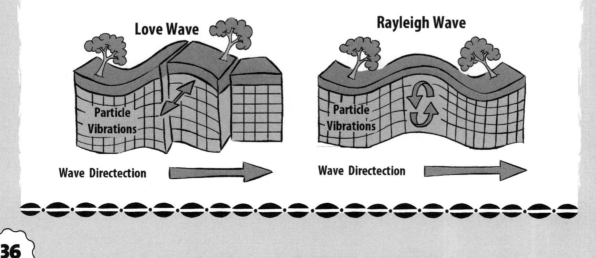

SAN ANDREAS FAULT SYSTEM

The San Andreas Fault is about 800 miles long (1,300 kilometers) and up to 10 miles deep (16 kilometers). It runs from just off the coast of northern California, south through California and into Mexico. The faults are positioned in a northwest to southeast direction.

The San Andreas Fault isn't really one fault at all, but a whole zone of parallel faults made up of many segments that are connected.

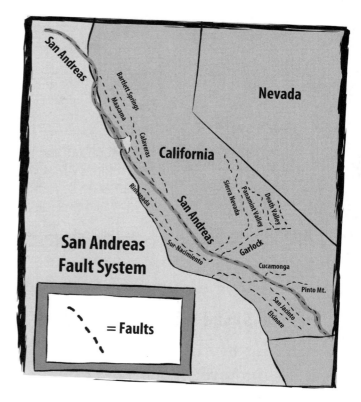

The San Andreas Fault System is a prime example of a transform fault system, where tectonic plates slide past each other. When this happens, the landscape is sheared into slivers of mountains with deep valleys between.

Did You Know?

Faults don't open during earthquakes—there's no hole you can fall into. The whole reason earthquakes occur is because faults get "locked up" due to friction until the two sides of the fault lurch into a new position. If the fault opened up, there would be no friction. Sometimes there can be a shallow opening in the earth after an earthquake because of a landslide.

The San Andreas Fault is called a right lateral fault because if you could look down on the land from above, the land on the right side moves down relative to the land on the left side. Another way of putting it is that if you're standing on one side of the fault and look across the fault, the other side moves to the right. A left lateral fault moves in the opposite way, with the other side of the fault moving left.

TRY THIS!

Hold a deck of cards in front of you with each hand on either side of the deck, with your fingers pointed up and your thumbs pointed towards you. Your right hand is the North American Plate, and your left hand is the Pacific Plate. Slowly move your left hand up and your right hand down. Do the cards slide past each other? All of those cards sliding past each other are like a broad zone of faults in the San Andreas. You can see that there isn't just one fault, but many.

SAN FRANCISCO EARTHQUAKE OF 1906

In the early morning of April 18, 1906 in San Francisco, California, the earth shook powerfully for 40 seconds. Jesse Cook said "the whole street was undulating. It was as if the waves of the ocean were coming toward me, and billowing as they came." Quakes came 26 more times that day. San Francisco sits on top of the San Andreas Fault.

On that day, the San Andreas Fault experienced an earthquake that was one of the most devastating in the history of the United States.

Over 3,000 people died. Buildings were destroyed and the ground heaved and cracked. Trees swayed and broke.

Did You Know?

An earthquake in 1989 in San Francisco along the San Andreas Fault measured 6.9 on the **Richter scale**. The Marina District in the city was built on land that had been filled in with sand, soil, and other materials, but it was saturated with groundwater. When the earthquake hit, the sandy soil suffered liquefaction and numerous buildings shook violently and collapsed.

In some places, ground on one side of the fault moved as much as 16 feet in relation to the ground on the other side of the fault (5 meters).

WORDS TO KNOW

Richter scale: a scale used to measure the strength of an earthquake. When the measurement increases by 1, the strength of the earthquake increases by 10.

natural gas: a colorless, odorless gas that is used as a fuel.

The earthquake was intense over a wide area, including most of California and parts of Nevada and Oregon, but San Francisco was hit the worst. Most of the damage there was from fires that started because pipes carrying **natural gas** broke. Natural gas is highly flammable. A major pipeline of water from San Andreas Lake to San Francisco was broken, so the city didn't have water to put the fires out.

If you visit Point Reyes National Seashore, you can see evidence of the 1906 earthquake. There's a barn that's sitting on top of the San Andreas Fault, and a fence that broke and moved 16 feet (5 meters).

Did You Know?

The largest recorded earthquake in the world was in Chile on May 22, 1960. It measured 9.5 on the Richter scale. Seismographs all over the world recorded the seismic waves for several days. The entire earth was shaking!

WHAT DOES AN EARTHQUAKE FEEL LIKE?

Here are some typical effects that people might feel near the epicenter of earthquakes of various magnitudes. The epicenter is the point on the earth's surface that is directly above the location of an earthquake.

Magnitude on the Richter Scale	What it Feels Like	How Often They Occur in the World
Below 3.0	People usually can't feel it.	1,000 per day
3.0 to 3.9	People can feel a slight trembling, but there is no damage.	Over 100 per day
4.0 to 4.9	Tables and chairs rattle.	About 20 per day
5.0 to 6.9	Some damage to buildings, especially if they're poorly built.	About 3 per day
7.0 to 7.9	Serious damage to buildings, with some destroyed.	18 per year
8.0 to 8.9	Serious damage for several hundred miles.	1 per year
9.0 to 9.9	Devastating, affecting people for thousands of miles.	1 per 20 years
10.0 and up	Never recorded.	?

MAKE YOUR OWN
LIQUEFACTION

SUPPLIES

- metal loaf pan
- sand
- legos
- water
- large spoon
- clay or soil

1 Fill the loaf pan with sand, almost to the top. Pour in water to just below the surface of the sand. Make a building out of legos a few inches tall (about 8 centimeters) and about an inch wide (2½ centimeters). Place your lego building in the middle of the pan, about 1 inch deep in the sand (2½ centimeters).

2 Place the pan on a table. Tap the side of the pan repeatedly using the large spoon. The taps should be gentle, but as fast as you can make them. Watch what happens to the sand and the lego building.

3 Try the experiment with clay or soil. In which material does the lego building collapse first?

What's Happening?

When soil is loose and sandy, and then saturated with water, the water fills the gaps between the grains of sand. Under normal conditions the grains still touch each other so the sand is firm and can support buildings. In an earthquake the sand is briefly suspended in the water. This is called liquefaction, because the sandy soil behaves like a liquid. Buildings can tilt or sink into the squishy soil.

41

MAKE YOUR OWN
EARTHQUAKE WAVES

1 Set the Slinky on a table. You and your friend each grab an end and stretch the Slinky between you. Quickly push your hand forward, then back. You'll see a wave in the Slinky where a pack of rings are close to each other. The wave moves from you to your friend then back.

2 Stop the Slinky, then move your hand right and left horizontally. This time, the wave moves along the length of the Slinky, but the Slinky moves back and forth horizontally.

3 Lift the Slinky above the table, stretched between you. Move one end of the Slinky up and down. What does this wave look like?

SUPPLIES

- Slinky
- table
- a friend

What's Happening?

Notice in the first example that the wave moves in the same direction as the Slinky rings—directly from you to your friend. This kind of wave is called a pressure wave, or P wave. In the second and third examples, the Slinky is moving at right angles to the direction of the wave from you to your friend. This kind of wave is called a shear wave, or S wave.

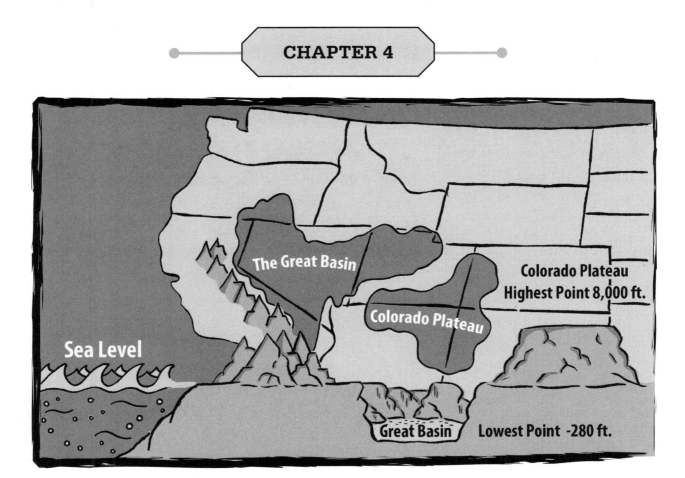

CHAPTER 4

PLATEAUS, PLAINS, BASINS

From the Colorado Plateau and the **Great Basin**, to the plains of Texas and Oklahoma, the Desert Southwest has some amazing, flat expanses of land.

WORDS TO KNOW

Great Basin: a large area covering most of Nevada, half of Utah, and bits of Idaho, Wyoming, Oregon, and California. All precipitation drains inward to the basin, with no rivers flowing to the ocean.

Some are fairly high in elevation, like the Colorado Plateau, while others are close to sea level, like the coastal plains. Some are even below sea level, like parts of the Great Basin. But just because they're relatively flat, doesn't mean these areas aren't interesting. There's a lot going on!

43

hoodoo: a geologic formation in the shape of a spire, usually with varying thickness.

COLORADO PLATEAU: AN ISLAND OF CALM

Where can you find **hoodoos**, fins, goblins, and slot canyons? In the red rock country of the Colorado Plateau. This is a land where rocks rule, with towering landforms and deep canyons, but little water and vegetation. It's perhaps the best-known area of the Desert Southwest. The Colorado Plateau has the greatest concentration of National Parks of any other region in the United States. It sits relatively high in elevation and covers the corners of Utah, Colorado, New Mexico, and Arizona.

The rocks in the Colorado Plateau formed over many hundreds of millions of years. The oldest rocks record when the continent was being put together about 2 billion years ago.

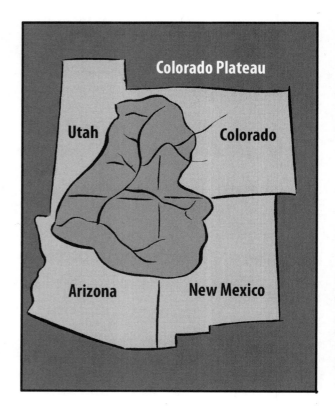

Tectonic plates were colliding and forming new volcanic islands. These islands smashed onto the North American continent, causing the continent to grow southward. Some rocks were buried and heated, and other rocks formed from deposited sediments. It was a crazy time! You can see these rocks at the very bottom of the Grand Canyon.

There is a large gap in time when the rocks that formed next were later eroded. But for most of the rest of that time, the area was relatively quiet. The region was much lower than today, and shallow inland seas filled the area, much like the Mediterranean Sea in Europe today. The seas rose and fell, leaving sediments like sand, mud, and limy mud that became layers of rock called sandstone, shale, and limestone.

**Date of Formation
(millions of years ago)**

65

146

208

245

270

290

320

360

540

1,050

Then, about 65 million years ago, the Colorado Plateau began to be pushed up to about a mile high in elevation (1½ kilometers). All around the Colorado Plateau land was deformed—from the Rocky Mountains to the Basin and Range Region. But the Colorado Plateau was only mildly deformed. It has remained fairly stable, with little folding and faulting.

Because of this, the layers of sedimentary rock in most areas of the Colorado Plateau look like a layer cake, with one flat layer of rock on top of another. And as the region has risen, streams and rivers have cut down through these layers in their journey to the ocean. This cutting has carved canyons like nowhere else on Earth!

President Theodore Roosevelt called the Grand Canyon "the one great sight which every American should see." And it's true—the Grand Canyon is amazing, both for its beauty and in the incredible record of rock history visible for all to see.

Like the rest of the Colorado Plateau, the rocks that we see in the Grand Canyon took a long time to form. They represent about 1,600 million years of history. The river itself took far less time to cut the canyon—at most 55 million years, and probably much less. How did the canyon become so deep and wide?

WORDS TO KNOW

Colorado River: the river that carved the Grand Canyon and flows at its bottom. The Colorado stretches 1,400 miles from the Rocky Mountains to the Gulf of Mexico (2,250 kilometers), and drops over 14,000 feet (4,267 meters).

It might seem strange in such a dry area, but the canyon formed from the erosive power of water. The **Colorado River** carved the channel itself and carries away sediment. In general, the higher in elevation a river is, the more power it has to carve a channel. Rivers that don't drop much in elevation, like the Mississippi, are "lazy" rivers that slowly wind back and forth. But rivers that have a large drop in elevation are faster moving and carve narrow, deep channels. The Grand Canyon sits very high—thousands of feet above sea level—so the Colorado River has a lot of energy to carve its channel.

A different source of water caused the canyon to be wide: rain. In wet climates, there's a lot more vegetation, and soil forms. The soil is continually creeping downslope, so the landscape tends to have rounded forms. In dry climates like the Grand Canyon's, the rain that does come is from short, violent storms. There isn't much vegetation or soil to absorb the rain, so the storms cause flash floods.

Most of the time there isn't much erosion of the sides of the canyon, but when there is, the floods can carry rocks and even large boulders down into the main channel. The Colorado River then carries those rocks and boulders downstream and out of the canyon.

ARCHES NATIONAL PARK

Along the road that climbs into Arches National Park, it seems as if you're entering another planet. The sandstone rock is red, stark, and forms sheer cliffs. Some of those cliffs form arches of all shapes and sizes. How did these beautiful shapes form?

Deep beneath the surface is a very thick layer of salt. The weight of the overlying rocks caused the salt to flow somewhat, almost like a liquid. This caused the rocks to shift and crack, pushing some areas up and others down. Eventually all of this movement shaped the sandstone rocks into a series of relatively thin "fins." They look a bit like a bunch of sailfish swimming along side by side, with only their fins above water. Many of these fins have eroded away completely, but others just eroded through the center, forming an arch.

Did You Know?

Arches National Park contains over 2,000 natural arches. This is the greatest number of natural arches in one area in the world. It contains many famous rock arches and formations, including Delicate Arch, Double Arch, Landscape Arch, and Balanced Rock.

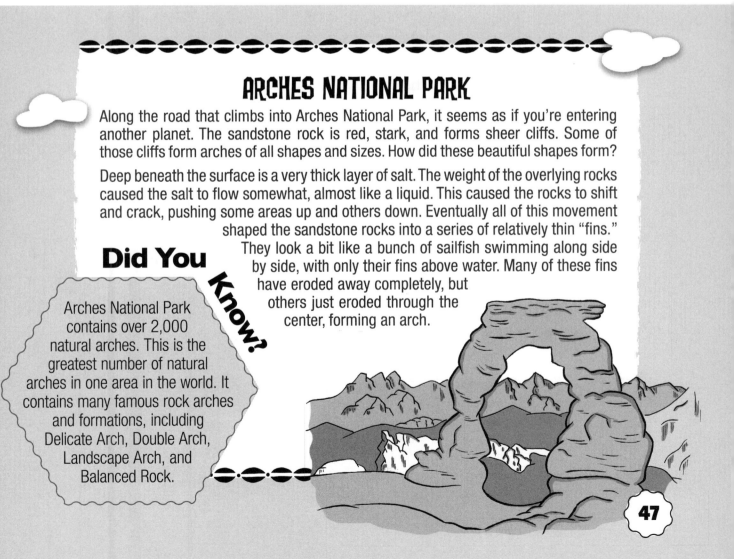

47

Did You Know?

If you imagine the history of the earth happening in one year, the oldest rocks in the Grand Canyon would have formed on August 10, the limestone layer of rock at the top of the Grand Canyon would have formed on December 10, and the canyon itself would have been carved somewhere between the afternoon of December 27 and December 31.

One mystery that geologists are still figuring out is that the canyon cuts through an area called the Kaibab Uplift. This area has a slight dome shape.

If the Colorado River had flowed in its present course from the beginning, it would have flowed up and over the Kaibab Uplift. Of course, this is impossible because water doesn't ever flow uphill.

Geologists used to think that the Colorado flowed in its present course from east to west, and the area in the Kaibab Uplift was pushed up at exactly the same rate as the river was cutting down. Slow and steady. It's a bit like cutting a layer cake by holding the knife steady above the cake, and lifting the cake up "through" the knife.

Most scientists don't see such a simple picture anymore, though. There is evidence that the uplift began much earlier than most parts of the canyon formed. Maybe one or more earlier canyons formed in different places and at different times, and they were then linked together at the Kaibab Uplift to form the Grand Canyon we know today. One thing is certain: geologists will keep working to find the answers.

SLOT CANYONS

Slot canyons are canyons that are much narrower than they are deep—sometimes only 1 foot wide (less than ½ meter)! They form by water carving through the rock. Walking through them can feel like walking into another world, with vertical walls of stone rising on either side.

Utah has more slot canyons than anywhere else in the world. Buckskin Gulch, Utah, is 13 miles long (21 kilometers), the longest slot canyon in the world, with a narrow, twisting path. Zion National Park has a section of its canyon called the Narrows, carved by the Virgin River. The Narrows is up to about 2,000 feet deep (610 meters) and in places only 20 feet wide (6 meters). When you hike the Narrows, you follow the river and often have to wade in the river itself, surrounded by sheer, red walls. In places you have to wade chest-deep!

Slot canyons can be treacherous during thunderstorm season. Even if skies are blue overhead, thunderstorms far upriver can send torrents of water through the canyons. These flash floods can rise in just minutes, with a wall of water 12 feet high or more (3½ meters). And because the walls are so high, you might have to hike miles before you can find a place to climb out of the canyon.

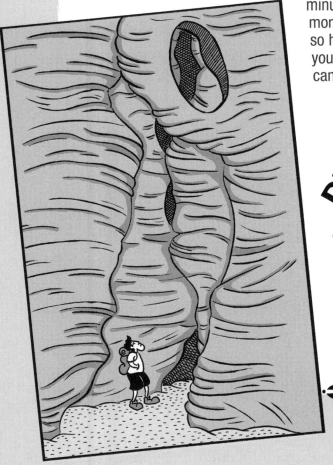

Did You Know?

Bryce Canyon National Park and other areas on the Colorado Plateau are home to tall, skinny spires of rock called hoodoos or goblins. Hoodoos can be as tall as a 10-story building. Many have their own name, such as Thor's Hammer, the Rabbit, or the Hunter.

Did You Know?

The plains of Texas and Oklahoma formed in a similar fashion to the other plains and plateaus in the region, with shallow, inland seas depositing sediments. Along the Gulf Coast, vast amounts of sediments have been deposited more recently, which actually presses the crust downward towards the shore. The plains are fertile land for growing crops and grazing cattle.

Large areas on the Colorado Plateau are a work of art called the Painted Desert. From a distance, the Painted Desert looks like colorful, striped powder puffs, soft and fluffy.

Red, blue, and green rocks form beautiful stripes. The Painted Desert also looks old, like it's been eroding forever. Not so! The soft layers only began eroding recently, about 6 to 15 million years ago.

The Painted Desert layers formed when mud mixed with volcanic ash changed to clay. The beautiful colors come from minerals contained in the rocks and the conditions present when they were formed. Some of the clay is capped by rock that's harder and resists erosion. Once erosion breaks through that capstone, though, the clays underneath erode very quickly. When it rains, the clay expands—it can absorb seven times its volume in water!

When it dries, the surface cracks so much that it's called "elephant skin."

It is extremely difficult for plants to take root, and, with no plants, the clay erodes easily. Heavy rains in the summer remove as much as a quarter inch of rock each year (½ centimeter). That may not seem like much, but in 100 years, up to 2 feet can erode (½ meter). The rain also forms gullies in the rocks, creating the soft, rounded shapes.

THE GREAT BASIN

The Great Basin gets its name because it acts like a large basin, or bowl, for precipitation. All of the precipitation drains inward—no rivers flow from the Great Basin to the ocean. Water that falls in the Great Basin, stays in the Great Basin. The region doesn't get very much precipitation to begin with, and it either evaporates off right away, sinks into the ground, or flows into lakes. Most of those lakes have a high salt content, like Great Salt Lake.

The Great Basin is a huge, low-lying area that covers most of Nevada, half of Utah, and bits of Idaho, Wyoming, Oregon, and California.

SHIPROCK

Shiprock is a huge rock formation that resembles a ship. It soars 1,100 feet above the surrounding plain on the Navajo Nation in western New Mexico (335 meters). This rock used to be the inner part of a much larger volcanic mountain. The rest of the mountain has eroded away, just leaving this remnant. Shiprock is a sacred site for the Navajo people.

51

Even though the Great Basin is low in elevation, within it there is a huge range in elevation, from 4,000 to 13,000 feet (1,200 to 4,000 meters). Most of the rocks formed in a similar environment as the rocks on the Colorado Plateau. Sediments like sand, mud, and clay were laid down in shallow seas. Layers and layers of sediments turned into sedimentary rocks.

The Great Basin is part of an even larger region called the Basin and Range Province. The Great Basin is 200,000 square miles (518,000 square kilometers) in area—as big as the 14 smallest states in the United States combined! Really, it is made up of about 100 smaller basins. It contains the Great Basin Desert, which is one of the four deserts found in the United States.

Did You Know?

The lowest point in North America is Badwater Basin, located in the Great Basin in Death Valley National Park. It's 280 feet below sea level (85 meters)!

VISIT OUTER SPACE . . . IN NORTHERN ARIZONA

About 50,000 years ago a massive meteorite slammed into Earth. It was about 150 feet across (46 meters) and weighed about 300,000 tons (272,155 metric tons). It was traveling so fast—26,000 miles per hour (41,843 kilometers)—that when it hit, it caused an explosion with 1,000 times more force than the first nuclear bombs. In just a few seconds, this massive explosion made a big hole in the earth called a crater. The crater was 700 feet deep (213 meters) and 4,000 feet across (1,220 meters).

Because of the dry climate, the crater hasn't eroded much, and it's considered the world's best-preserved meteor crater. The moon has many more craters than Earth, and Apollo astronauts trained here, at Meteor Crater, in preparation for moonwalks.

The web site for Meteor Crater has a video of what the meteorite impact might have looked like: www.meteorcrater.com.

MESA VERDE

Carved into spectacular sandstone canyons in southern Colorado are over 600 cliff dwellings. Native Americans called Anasazi built these dwellings from about 1,400 to 700 years ago. The overhanging cliffs in the sandstone provided the perfect place to build these complicated, interconnected houses and villages.

The area should really be called "Cuesta Verde." A cuesta is a cliff that gently slopes. A mesa has a steep slope. At Mesa Verde, the gentle, 7-degree slope of the cliffs makes an ideal alcove for the dwellings.

MAKE YOUR OWN
EGG-CRACKING EXPERIMENT

1 Take off any rings on your fingers, and try to crush an egg in the palm of one hand. Make sure to hold your hand over the sink. Can you do it? If it breaks, be sure to wash up carefully.

2 Now take the clay and form six small balls. Push your finger into the center of each ball so that it forms an indentation. Fit the clay onto the top and bottom of each of the three remaining eggs.

3 Place the three eggs onto the cookie sheet in the shape of a triangle with equal sides, with the narrow end of the eggs facing up. Place the second cookie sheet on top of the eggs.

SUPPLIES

- 4 raw eggs
- piece of modeling clay or play clay
- 2 cookie sheets
- heavy books
- paper towels

4 Place heavy books on the cookie sheet, one at a time. How many books will the eggs hold before breaking? Was it more or fewer than you expected? Take a piece of eggshell and crack it between your fingers. How does that compare in strength to the entire egg?

5 Wipe up all of the broken egg with paper towels, then wash your hands.

6 You can also try this as a trick with friends. First make sure they don't have any rings on, but wear a ring yourself. They probably won't be able to crush the egg. With a ring, you should be able to if you squeeze very hard.

What's Happening?

The arch shape is one of the strongest in nature, especially for holding weights. Some materials, like stone, are very strong when they're being squeezed, or compressed, but not so strong when they're stretched. Arches direct pressure, or weight, so that it squeezes the material along the lines of the arch. Eggs have a natural arch shape, and so do natural bridges and arches. They're both very strong when they're squeezed or have weight on top of them. Look around you. Do you see this arch structure in buildings or bridges?

MAKE YOUR OWN
MINI-CANYON

1 Roll out two colors of clay about ¼ inch thick (½ centimeter). Stack the layers of clay onto the cardboard. These are like the layers of rock.

2 With the layers flat on the table, push from both sides. If the clay sticks to the cardboard, lift the middle up into at least one fold. Your hands are like the forces from two continents pushing on rocks. The middle is a fold.

3 Holding the wire taut, use it like a knife to make a cut through the top part of the folded layers, parallel to the table. You should see the underneath layer showing through. This is like the forces of erosion leveling off a surface.

SUPPLIES

- at least 5 colors of play clay
- rolling pin
- cardboard about 12 inches square (30 centimeters)
- thin wire
- blue yarn or embroidery thread *(optional)*

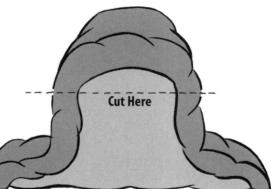

Cut Here

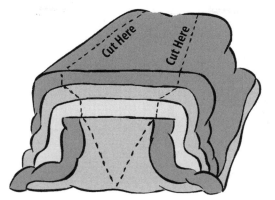

4 Roll out the other colors of clay about ½-inch thick (1 centimeter). Stack them on top of the folded clay.

5 Choose a direction for the "river" to run through the clay. It should be at an angle to how your hands were placed. Run your fingernail lightly across the top to show where the river will run.

6 On either side of the "river" make two vertical cuts parallel to the river and through the top layer of clay until you reach the next layer. Peel away the slab of clay to reveal the next layer of clay underneath. This top layer is a cliff-forming layer of rock.

7 On the next layer, make two cuts at an angle; this is a slope-forming layer of rock. Place the wire at the bottom of the top layer and pull it down and towards the river until you reach the next layer. Repeat on the other side of the river, then peel away this layer.

8 Continue cutting away layers, alternating cliffs and slopes until you reach the lowest folded rocks. Make a V-shaped cut through the folded layers, almost to the cardboard. If you'd like, cut a piece of blue yarn and place it at the bottom of the "V" to be the Colorado River.

CHAPTER 5

CLIMATE

The Desert Southwest is marked by what it lacks: water. Most areas receive less than 10 inches (25 centimeters) of precipitation each year. This affects the plants, animals, soil, rivers, and even the shape of the land itself. You might think of the Desert Southwest as being very hot, and it can be. But it can also be quite cold. Why is the climate of this region so different from the rest of the United States? Grab a canteen of water, and let's go find out!

HOW DRY IS IT?

The western sides of the Coastal Mountains and the Sierra Nevada in California receive plenty of rain each year. But cross over the Sierra Nevada, and you come to the driest place in North America: Death Valley National Park. How can that be?

It's because of the mountains. As warm air passes over the oceans, it picks up moisture. In the United States, the winds tend to blow from west to east. When the warm, moist air from the ocean hits the West Coast, the mountains force the air up along the slopes. When air rises,

WORDS TO KNOW

rain shadow: an area that is dry because it is on the side of a mountain away from the wind.

it cools. Colder air can hold less water vapor than warmer air. So the water vapor in the air condenses into tiny droplets and forms clouds. Have you ever seen clouds covering the tops of mountains? If enough water vapor condenses into droplets, it rains.

As the air passes over the mountains and descends the other side, it warms. The air has lost some of its moisture from raining. It also can hold more water vapor because it is warmer. So the far side of the mountains has much less rainfall. This is called a **rain shadow**. There is a rain shadow for the entire Desert Southwest because of the Coast Mountains and the Sierra Nevada. That makes the air feel dry, and there's little rain.

Cool Air

Moist Air Rises

Dry Air Falls

Warm Air

WORDS TO KNOW

Northern Hemisphere: the half of the earth north of the equator.

monsoon: a wind system that brings heavy rains for one part of the year, and almost no rain the rest of the year.

From the Gulf Coast on the eastern side of the Southwest, moisture-rich air sweeps onto the coast of Texas. There is a lot of rain in east Texas. But because winds and storms tend to go from west to east in the **Northern Hemisphere**, the storms usually move north from there instead of west. So most of the Southwest doesn't receive much moisture from the Atlantic Ocean either.

MONSOONS!

You may have heard of **monsoons** occurring around West Africa or Asia, especially in India. Monsoons are wind systems that bring heavy rains for one part of the year. They occur because in the summer, the air over land heats much faster than the air over oceans. When the warmer air over the land rises, cooler air from over the ocean moves in toward the land to take its place. Air over oceans carries a lot of water vapor, which means it dumps a lot of rain as it moves over the land. In the winter, the pattern reverses, and drier air over land moves out to the ocean. The rain carried by the summer monsoon winds can be tremendous, with up to 390 inches of rain each year in parts of India (almost 1,000 centimeters).

Much of the Southwest also experiences monsoons, but with much less rain. They vary quite a bit in how much rain they carry, and where the rain falls. Almost half of the annual precipitation in many areas falls in the summer months of July, August, and September. This is because the land over Mexico and the southwest United States heats up and rises. Air from the Gulf of California and the Gulf of Mexico moves in, carrying moisture with it. Just as residents of New Mexico or Arizona think they can't take the heat anymore, a monsoon thunderstorm is likely to break overhead, bringing welcome rain and cooler air.

WORDS TO KNOW

latitude: the lines that run west and east on the globe parallel to the equator. Latitudes vary from zero degrees at the equator to 90 degrees at the North and South Poles.

IS IT HOT?
WHAT MAKES IT HOT?

Much of the American desert is hot, but there are colder temperatures at times than you might expect. What makes it hot, yet also sometimes quite cold?

The sun is the main source of heat in any climate. The biggest factor in how much energy the earth receives from the sun is the angle at which the sun's rays hit the ground. When the sun is high in the sky, then the rays hit directly. But when the sun is low in the sky, the rays hit at an angle, and the same energy is spread out over a larger area. That's why you feel more heat from the sun at noon than just before the sun sets. Places that are near the equator, at a low **latitude**, get very direct sunlight and are hot.

12 PM

9 AM

3 PM

7 AM

5 PM

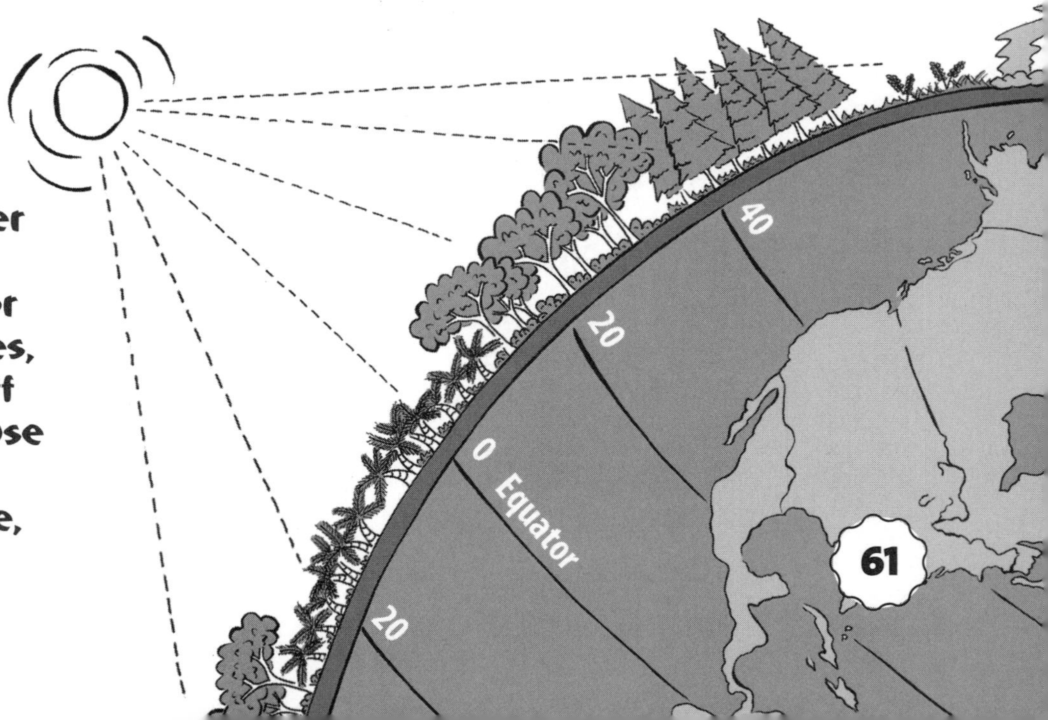

As you go farther north or south from the equator to higher latitudes, the sun gives off less energy because its rays hit at more of an angle, so it's colder.

40

20

0 Equator

20

61

Like nearly all of the United States, the Desert Southwest is located more or less midway between the equator and the North Pole. This is called the temperate zone, which means that weather varies quite a bit from season to season, with hot and cold weather. The Desert Southwest is on the southern end of the temperate zone, though, so it's somewhat closer to the equator. That makes it hotter.

WORDS TO KNOW

diurnal temperature difference: the difference in temperatures between the day and night. Deserts tend to have large diurnal temperature differences.

Did You Know?

Yuma, Arizona, is the sunniest city in an average year in the United States. It experiences on average 4,300 hours of sunlight each year. During June, the sun shines 97 percent of the daylight hours in Yuma. The top five sunniest states in the United States are all in the Desert Southwest—Arizona, California, Nevada, New Mexico, and Texas.

Because there are usually very few clouds, deserts experience big temperature differences between night and day. This is called the **diurnal temperature difference**. During the day, the sunlight isn't blocked by clouds, so it heats the earth quickly. Clouds would act as a "blanket" to keep in heat at night. Without clouds, the earth loses its heat quickly during the night. The result? Many parts of the Southwest have diurnal temperature differences of 30 degrees Fahrenheit (17 degrees Celsius).

WEATHER AND CLIMATE: WHAT'S THE DIFFERENCE?

People often get weather and climate confused. Weather is what happens in the atmosphere related to temperature, precipitation, winds, and clouds. Climate is the average weather of a place over a long period of time.

Elevation to Temperature

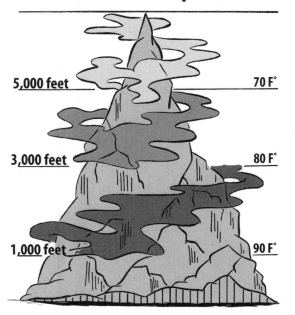

5,000 feet — 70 F°

3,000 feet — 80 F°

1,000 feet — 90 F°

The higher you go, the colder it becomes. This is because, like clouds, the atmosphere acts like a blanket to keep heat in. At higher elevations, there aren't as many air molecules, so the "blanket" isn't as thick and heat escapes. That's why even in the Desert Southwest, many high mountains are always covered in snow. It never gets warm enough up there for the snow to completely melt, even in the summer.

TRANSITION ZONES: TEXAS AND OKLAHOMA

Both Texas and Oklahoma have big differences between the climates in the western and eastern parts of the states. The western areas are dry, much like the rest of the Desert Southwest. But the eastern areas receive over 50 inches of annual rainfall (127 centimeters). Looking on a map, you might guess why: the eastern areas receive lots of rain from storms coming in from the Gulf of Mexico. These storms sweep in and travel mostly north into the Great Plains, dumping rain as they go.

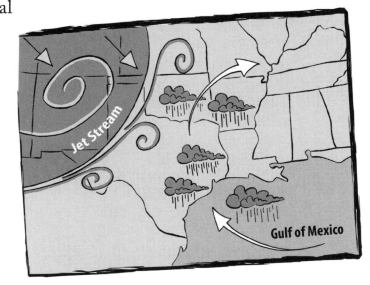

63

DEATH VALLEY . . . HOT AND DRY

Death Valley National Park, located in California and Nevada, has one of the most extreme climates on Earth: very hot and very dry.

HOW HOT? On July 10, 1913, the thermometer climbed to 134 degrees Fahrenheit (57 degrees Celsius). That's the hottest temperature ever recorded in North America, and, until 1922, in the world. In 2001, there were 154 days in a row that were 100 degrees Fahrenheit or above (38 degrees Celsius). And that's just the air. The ground gets much hotter: on July 15, 1972, the ground reached 201 degrees Fahrenheit (94 degrees Celsius). That's hot enough to fry an egg!

HOW DRY? Death Valley averages less than 2 inches of rain each year (5 centimeters). This has been a bit higher in the last 30 years. Compare that to Mobile, Alabama, which receives on average 67 inches of rain per year (170 centimeters). In 1929 and 1953, there was no rain recorded at all in Death Valley! But the rate of **evaporation** in the valley is up to 12 inches per year (30 centimeters). So any rain that does fall quickly evaporates.

WORDS TO KNOW

evaporation: the process where a liquid heats up and changes into a gas, such as water vapor.

WHY? Death Valley's climate is an extreme version of the rain shadow that makes the rest of the Southwest hot and dry. The Sierra Nevada mountains just to the west of Death Valley are quite high, but Death Valley is very low—282 feet below sea level (86 meters)! As air descends from the high mountains it's squeezed because of increased pressure. That makes lower elevations hotter than higher ones: temperatures rise up to 5 degrees Fahrenheit (3 degrees Celsius) with every 1,000-foot drop in elevation (305 meters). The shape of the land at Death Valley also affects the temperature. As the rocks and bare soil heat up on the dry desert floor, warm air rises. But Death Valley is surrounded by high mountains, so the hot air is trapped.

MAKE YOUR OWN
SOLAR OVEN

SUPPLIES

- 1 large box
- newspapers
- 1 medium pizza box
- cardboard
- clear packing tape
- aluminum foil
- black construction paper
- scissors
- clear rigid plastic, at least as big as the pizza box
- thermometer
- marshmallows
- chocolate

You should have an adult to help with this activity.

1 Fill the bottom of the large box with crumpled newspapers. Set the medium pizza box on top of the newspapers. The top of the pizza box should be level with the top of the large box. If it isn't, put more crumpled newspapers underneath the pizza box. Then place more crumpled newspapers in the spaces along the sides between the two boxes. The newspaper will act as insulation.

2 Place pieces of cardboard over the spaces between the boxes and tape securely.

3 Line the inside of the bottom section of the pizza box with aluminum foil and tape securely.

4 Place the black construction paper over the aluminum foil on the bottom of the pizza box and tape securely.

continues on next page . . .

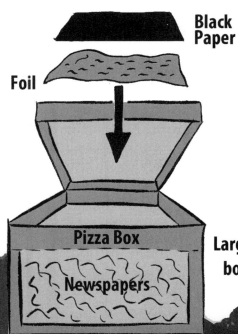

Black Paper

Foil

Pizza Box

Newspapers

Larger box

5 Draw a square on the top of the pizza box lid 1 inch from the edges (2½ centimeters). Cut along this square on three sides, but NOT on the side along the back of the box. Carefully lift the flap you have just cut. Tape aluminum foil to the inside of the flap.

6 Cut the plastic so that it is ¼ inch smaller than the pizza box all around (½ centimeter). Tape the plastic securely to the inside of the pizza box top so that there are no gaps between the plastic and the edges of the pizza box. The plastic will cover the hole left by the flap.

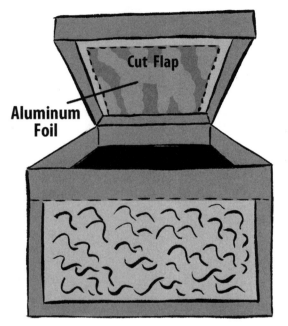

Cut Flap

Aluminum Foil

7 What do you want to cook? Maybe marshmallows and chocolate for s'mores? Place your solar cooker outside on a sunny day. Place the thermometer and the marshmallows on top of the black paper and close the top.

8 Prop the flap open so the aluminum foil reflects sunlight into the box. You should be able to see your marshmallows through the clear plastic. When the marshmallows are almost cooked, add chocolate and watch it melt. Enjoy!

9 Check the temperature inside the pizza box. Now measure the temperature outside the pizza box, but still in the sun. How much did your pizza box heat things up?

Food

What's Happening?

Aluminum foil reflects light. Light waves bounce off the aluminum foil all around, including through the clear plastic and onto the marshmallows. Light also hits the marshmallows directly. The black paper absorbs the energy from the sun, helping to heat up the space inside the pizza box. The newspapers and plastic help to insulate your oven, so that heat does not escape.

Your oven should reach about 200 degrees Fahrenheit (93 degrees Celsius) on a sunny day. If it doesn't, check that everything is sealed well.

MAKE YOUR OWN
HOMEMADE ADOBE BRICKS

1 Sift the topsoil through the screen into a bucket. Break up the large chunks if you can. Discard any large rocks.

2 Mix the sifted soil and sand in the bucket. Use about two parts soil to one part sand. Stir in enough water to make a thick mud. The mud should be thick enough that you can roll some of it between your hands.

SUPPLIES

- topsoil from the garden or a garden center
- hardware cloth or screen with ¼ inch openings (½ centimeter)
- large bucket
- sand
- water
- 1 or more shoeboxes
- ice cube tray *(optional)*

Water

Soil
Sand

+

=

Adobe Mud

3 Pack the mud into one or more shoeboxes, each about two-thirds full. Smooth the top surface of the mud. Let the mud set for a day. You can also put mud into ice cube trays if you want to make bricks for a miniature house.

4 Flip the boxes over and slide the bricks out. Put them in a dry place out of the rain to dry for a few days. If you have several bricks, you can build a wall by using more mud between the bricks, just like mortar in a brick wall.

WORDS TO KNOW

adobe: brick made out of sun-dried clay and sometimes straw.

What's Happening?

Mud is one of the oldest building materials. People of the Southwest have been making mud bricks, called **adobe** bricks, for thousands of years. Because of the dry climate in the Southwest, there aren't a lot of trees providing wood, but there is a lot of clay.

MAKE YOUR OWN
SWAMP COOLER

Try this activity on a hot, dry day to cool off! An adult needs to help with the fan.

1 Select a location for your swamp cooler where drips are okay and where there's a railing. A porch is a good place. This will work best on a hot, dry, breezy day.

2 Soak the fabric in water and drape it over the railing. Stand in front of the damp fabric. Does the air feel cooler? If there's an adult to help, set up a fan so that it blows air through the burlap. You have to be very careful to keep any dripping water completely away from the fan and the electrical outlet.

SUPPLIES

- large piece of burlap or other fabric with a coarse weave
- water
- railing
- fan
- pitcher of water
- thermometer

WORDS TO KNOW

evaporative cooler: a device that blows air over a moist surface. As the water evaporates, it cools the air. Also called a swamp cooler.

3 Use the pitcher to periodically drip more water onto the burlap to keep it wet.

4 Set up a place inside where it's okay if water drips a little. To see how much the swamp cooler is cooling the room, record the room temperature before you do the project, then after the fan has been blowing for about an hour. Did it cool the room as much as you expected?

What's Happening?

When water evaporates, it absorbs heat from whatever is surrounding it, including the air. So as air blows over the moist fabric, the water evaporates and cools the air blowing through. Evaporative coolers don't work very well on humid days. This is because the air is already full of water vapor, so little water will evaporate.

Swamp coolers are used in cities like Albuquerque, New Mexico; Tucson and Phoenix, Arizona; El Paso, Texas; and Salt Lake City, Utah, where the humidity is low and temperatures are high. They work much like your homemade swamp cooler does, and they use much less electricity to operate than regular air conditioning.

Did You Know?

Your body is a natural **evaporative cooler**. When you sweat, the water evaporates and cools you off.

CHAPTER 6

RIVERS AND LAKES

Rivers are the lifeblood of any landscape. But in the Desert Southwest, where rain falls only now and then, rivers are truly a ribbon of life. Plants, animals, and people depend on the water in rivers to thrive and grow. Where there is water, there is also life. There are two major river systems in the Desert Southwest: the Colorado River and the Rio Grande.

WORDS TO KNOW

tributary: a stream or river that flows into a larger river.

watershed: the land area that drains into a river or stream.

The water in rivers comes from precipitation that flows over the surface of the land. Smaller creeks and streams flow together and form bigger streams and rivers. They are called **tributaries** of the larger river they flow into. The land that drains into a river is the **watershed** of that river. Most rivers flow into the ocean.

THE COLORADO RIVER

The mighty Colorado River begins 9,010 feet high (2,746 meters) in the lush valleys of Rocky Mountain National Park in Colorado. It travels through mountains and deserts, carving gorgeous canyons as it goes, including the Grand Canyon. After flowing through Utah and Arizona, it forms the border between Nevada and Arizona and between Arizona and California. Then it flows through Mexico into the Gulf of California. Its watershed drains parts of seven states and Mexico. At over 1,400 miles long (2,253 kilometers), the Colorado River is the third-longest river in the lower 48 states.

Most of the time, the Colorado never even reaches the ocean because it's just a dry streambed at the Gulf. The water has been used up by people, agriculture, and evaporation.

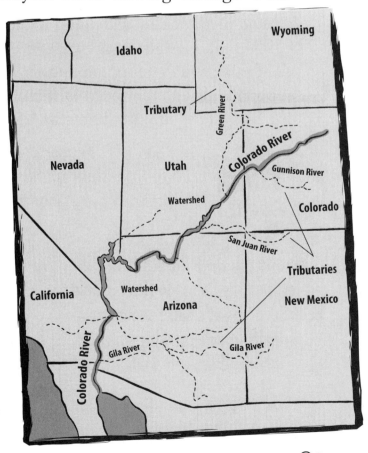

ALL-AMERICAN CANAL

The All-American Canal is the largest canal in the world, carrying more water than New York's Hudson River! It carries water 80 miles (129 kilometers) from the Colorado River to the Imperial Valley in California to **irrigate crops**. The Imperial Valley is in the Sonoran Desert and receives only about 3 inches of rain per year (8 centimeters). But about half of all people in the Imperial Valley make their living in agriculture. Chances are, you've eaten fruits or vegetables grown in the Imperial Valley.

WORDS TO KNOW

irrigate: to supply land with water using pipes and ditches, usually for crops.

crops: plants grown for food and other uses.

Some of the cities that draw water from the Colorado River include Las Vegas, Nevada; Los Angeles, San Bernardino, and San Diego, California; and Phoenix and Tucson, Arizona. These cities are all growing in population and may need even more water from the river in the future. The biggest use of water from the Colorado is for growing crops.

Think About It!

How do you think the rights to use water from the Colorado River should be divided? What's more important— growing crops, drinking water, watering lawns, or wildlife?

People don't always agree about who has the right to use the water from the Colorado. There have been many lawsuits over how much water each state can use. The Colorado River Compact was established in 1922 to work out an agreement about water rights along different sections of the river. Native Americans have claims to its water too, and the water needs of wildlife also must be met. The Colorado River provides water for millions of people, plants, and animals.

HYDROELECTRIC ENERGY

All along the Colorado River, the energy from flowing water is turned into electricity. The Colorado River starts high in elevation, so it's relatively steep with lots of energy from the flowing water. Hydro means water, so a **hydroelectric plant** makes electricity from the energy of water.

hydroelectric plant: a power plant that changes the energy from flowing water into electricity.

Hydroelectric energy works by using the flowing water to turn large turbines. These are like water wheels on their sides. The rotating turbine blades cause huge magnets to spin very fast, which creates electricity. To control how the water flows through the turbines, dams have been built to hold back the water in large areas called reservoirs. There are about 20 major dams on the Colorado and its tributaries. Their large reservoirs include Lake Mead and Lake Powell.

HOOVER DAM

When the Hoover Dam was built in 1936 on the Colorado River's border between Nevada and Arizona, it was the highest dam in the world—726 feet high (221 meters). It's still the second-highest dam in the United States. The Hoover Dam supplies water and power to Nevada, Arizona, and California. It holds back the Colorado River to form a reservoir called Lake Mead, which is the largest reservoir in the United States. There's enough concrete in the Hoover Dam to pave a road from San Francisco, California, to New York City, New York. At its base, it's as thick as two football fields measured end to end!

THE RIO GRANDE

The Rio Grande also begins high in the Rocky Mountains, at about 12,000 feet in the San Juan Range in Colorado (3,658 meters). It flows south through New Mexico, then at El Paso it forms the border between Texas and Mexico before it flows into the Gulf of Mexico.

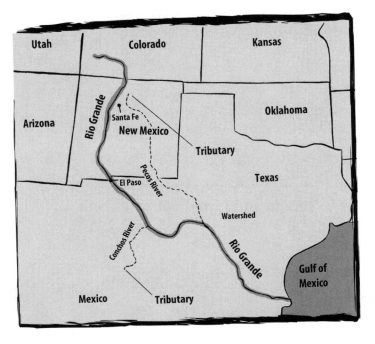

In Mexico, the river is called the Rio Bravo. Through most of its course, the Rio Grande flows through desert regions and is the center of life.

Like the Colorado River, the Rio Grande is used for drinking water, agriculture, and industry, especially in its lower section. For about 1,000 miles, it's an international border between the United States and Mexico, with major cities on each side. Alfalfa, pecans, peppers, and citrus fruits are grown all along the border.

Where it enters the Gulf of Mexico, the green, algae-filled water of the river mixes with the blue of the ocean. The river here is only about 20 feet wide (6 meters) because most of the water has been used upstream. In some years, the river doesn't quite reach the Gulf of Mexico.

Did You Know?

Spanish explorers used the Rio Grande as a "highway" in the New World, traveling north along the river to Santa Fe, New Mexico.

BIG BEND NATIONAL PARK

WORDS TO KNOW

species: a group of plants or animals that are closely related and look the same.

nutrients: substances that living things need to live and grow.

endangered: when a species is in danger of going extinct, so that it no longer exists anywhere.

As the Rio Grande winds its way towards the Gulf of Mexico, it takes a "big bend" in Texas from heading southeast to northeast. If you travel the river here by boat, you'll pass through 1,500-foot-high sheer vertical cliffs of limestone (457 meters). The entire area, which includes 240 miles of the United States–Mexico border (386 kilometers), is set aside as Big Bend National Park.

Big Bend is the largest protected area of the Chihuahua Desert. It's home to over 1,200 **species** of plants and a large variety of animals, including 75 species of mammals. There are snakes, bats, black bears, deer, javelina, coyote, and even mountain lions!

One of the most interesting animals in the park is the turkey vulture. They have red-skinned heads with no feathers, and long, bare legs. Turkey vultures eat dead things. And they poop on themselves to cool off. So you may not want to invite them for dinner.

But in the air, turkey vultures are gorgeous. They have a 6-foot wing span (2 meters). Since they weigh less than 5 pounds (2 kilograms), they can soar up to 40 miles per hour on warm drafts of air (64 kilometers per hour). You might see them early in the morning roosting on trees with their wings spread to warm up. Then later in the day they fly as high as 5,000 feet with little effort (1,524 meters). Turkey vultures are an important part of the ecosystem because they "clean" the desert of dead animals and recycle the **nutrients**.

Did You Know?

Big Bend National Park is the only place in the United States where the **endangered** Mexican long-nosed bat can be found.

77

BOSQUE DEL APACHE

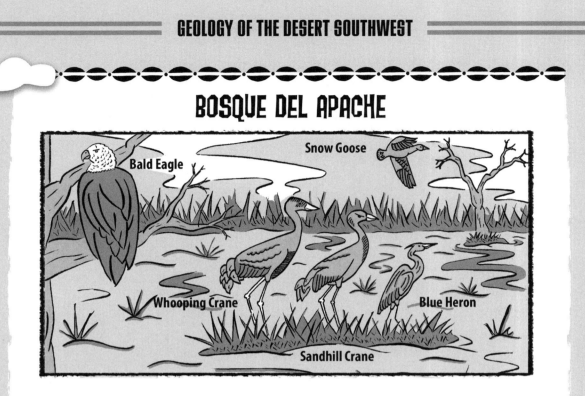

Bald Eagle
Snow Goose
Whooping Crane
Blue Heron
Sandhill Crane

The Bosque del Apache is a stretch of **wetlands** along the Rio Grande in central New Mexico. In the middle of the desert, it provides **habitat** for many animals, including deer, mountain lions, beaver, and porcupine. But it's probably best known for the birds that gather here in the winter in huge numbers. Over 370 species of birds visit the Bosque, **migrating** south to spend the winter here—song birds, shore birds, bald eagles, and blue herons. Tens of thousands of snow geese arrive, and as many as 28,000 sandhill cranes. There are even a few whooping cranes, the tallest North American bird and an endangered species.

Sandhill cranes have a wingspan of 6 to 8 feet (over 2 meters) and weigh up to 12 pounds (5 kilograms). They spend most of their time feeding, since they need to put on weight to have the energy to migrate north. Farmers plant corn and alfalfa in the Bosque, harvesting the alfalfa for themselves and leaving the corn for the birds.

There are few sights more beautiful than sandhill cranes swooping along the Bosque in the morning or evening in large numbers, or snow geese rising in "puffs" of thousands, where the air is so dense with birds you can't see the blue sky behind them.

WORDS TO KNOW

wetlands: an area where the land is saturated with water. Wetlands are important habitats for fish, plants, and wildlife.

habitat: a plant or animal's home.

migrate: to move from one region to another when the seasons change.

ACEQUIAS

There is a Spanish saying: "El agua es vida." Water is life. In the dry Southwest, this is particularly true. Over 400 years ago in 1598, Juan de Onate established the first permanent Spanish settlement in what is now New Mexico. The Spanish settlers constructed an irrigation ditch to bring water from the Rio Grande to fields planted with crops. The tradition of building and maintaining community ditches has continued to this day. These waterways are called **acequias**, a Spanish word for irrigation canals.

WORDS TO KNOW

acequia: a community-owned and operated irrigation waterway.

New Mexico has about 1,000 acequias, and most of them were dug when the Spanish first settled the area. The Acequia de Chamita in New Mexico dates back to around 1600 and is a National Historic Landmark. It is about 4 miles long (6½ kilometers) and irrigates land for about 83 families, most of whom are descended from the original Spanish settlers. The Acequia Associations—groups of people who use and maintain these community ditches—are considered the oldest democracies in the United States.

THE GREAT SALT LAKE

Imagine bobbing gently in the water like a cork, without even trying to float. That's what it's like at the Great Salt Lake in northern Utah. The saltiness ranges from 5 to 27 percent, compared to 3.5 percent in oceans. All that salt makes the water very dense and able to hold up objects—like you—easily. The northern arm of the lake is especially salty.

The Great Salt Lake is the largest saltwater lake in the Americas and the fourth-largest lake in the world that doesn't drain to the ocean. It's also the largest lake west of the Mississippi River. Normally, it's about 75 miles long and 35 miles wide (121 by 56 kilometers), but changes as the water level changes because the surrounding land is relatively flat.

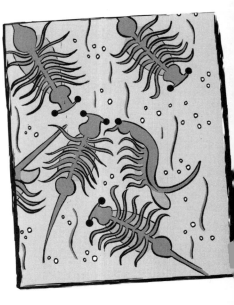

What made it so salty? The Great Salt Lake has no outlet to the ocean. It's in the Great Basin, where all precipitation drains to the interior. As rivers flow over the land, the water picks up salt and other minerals. When the water evaporates, the salts and minerals are left behind to slowly build up.

The lake is so salty that most fish can't live there. But tiny brine shrimp and brine flies thrive. Brine shrimp, also called sea monkeys, pump salt out through their gills, so the salt doesn't build up in their bodies. Also, baby brine shrimp only hatch at certain temperatures and salt levels.

There are many wetlands around the edges of the Great Salt Lake that are important stopping places for migrating birds. The birds' favorite food? All those brine shrimp and flies!

WORDS TO KNOW

groundwater: water that is underground in the spaces and cracks between sediments and rocks.

aquifer: a large area of groundwater.

xeriscaping: landscaping with plants that need less water.

UNDERGROUND LAKES?

A large area of **groundwater** is called an **aquifer**. When water falls as rain or snow and slowly seeps into the sediments or cracks in rocks, this is called recharge. Aquifers occur throughout the Southwest and often they are the only sources of drinking water.

Throughout the Basin and Range Region, aquifers are located in the basins between mountains, in layers of sediments beneath the surface. Some basins can have sediments up to 2 miles deep (3 kilometers), but the most easily accessible groundwater is only in the upper portion.

Ogallala Aquifer

The Ogallala Aquifer is located under west Texas and Oklahoma and the far eastern part of New Mexico, as well as under the southern Great Plains. It's one of the largest aquifers in the world. Many areas in the Southwest rely on groundwater for drinking, industry, and agriculture. The problem is that there isn't much rainfall, so the aquifers don't receive much recharge. When people pump more water out of aquifers than is being recharged, it's called "mining" water. The water level in the aquifer drops and it gets harder to pump. Sometimes the ground sinks.

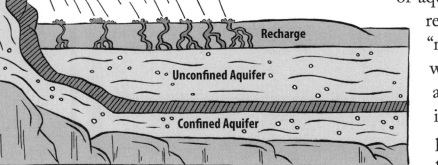

Albuquerque, New Mexico, relies completely on its aquifer for water. The Albuquerque Basin filled when the climate was colder and wetter, many thousands of years ago during the last Ice Age. The people who live there are trying to decrease the amount of water they use by installing shower heads, washing machines, and toilets that use less water. By **xeriscaping** their yards, they use less water for lawns and gardens.

MAKE YOUR OWN
AQUIFER

SUPPLIES

- 4 clear plastic cups the same size
- gravel
- coarse sand
- clay
- timer
- measuring cup
- water
- table knife

1 Fill one of the three cups to an inch below the rim with gravel (2½ centimeters). Fill the second cup with sand, and the third cup with clay. For the fourth cup, fill it half full with sand covered by one inch of clay, firmly packed. These are all sediments.

Gravel   Sand   Clay   Sand & Clay

2 Get your timer ready, then pour ¼ cup of water into the cup with gravel. Time how long it takes for the water to reach the bottom. Then do the same with the cups containing sand and clay. Which one takes the longest? Which one was fastest?

3 Look carefully at the water level in each cup. Keep adding water to each cup until the water level is even with the top of the sediment, making sure to measure and record how much water you pour in. If the water level is already above the top of the sediment, don't add additional water. Which type of sediment holds the most water?

4 Pour one-quarter cup of water into the cup with sand covered by clay. Does the water seep in? Take the table knife and make slices in the clay until you reach the sand. What happens now?

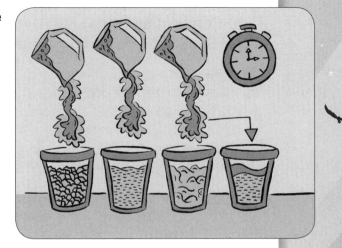

What's Happening?

Aquifers are underground rocks or sediments that hold water. When the sediments in an aquifer are smaller, they fit together more tightly and there isn't as much room for water in the spaces. So gravel holds more water, and the water flows through it faster than it flows through sand. When the particle size of the material is very small, as it is in clay, water can't move through it easily. When clay covers sediments underneath, like in the fourth cup, the sediments are called a confined aquifer. When this happens, rain and snow can only seep down into the aquifer if there are openings in the confining layer.

Did You Know?

The water in the Albuquerque Aquifer below about 500 feet deep (152 meters) is 18,000 to 20,000 years old!

MAKE YOUR OWN
SALTY LAKE

1 Fill the bowl with tap water. Add a spoonful of salt and stir until it is dissolved. Does the water taste salty?

2 Place the bowl in a warm, sunny place. Let it sit for several days, until the water level drops so the bowl is only about a quarter full. Stir the water and taste it. Does it taste more or less salty than it did before?

3 Let the water sit in the sunny spot until it completely evaporates. What happened to the salt?

4 Don't rinse the bowl, but add water until the bowl is half full, then add enough water each day so the level stays half full. How much water do you have to add to keep the level the same? If you move the bowl out of the sun, does this affect how much water you have to add? Does the water still taste salty?

SUPPLIES
- medium-sized bowl
- warm water
- salt
- spoon
- warm, sunny place

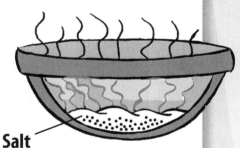

Evaporating Water

Salt

What's Happening

Just like the Great Salt Lake, when water evaporates, salt is left behind. Over time the salt levels build up.

Did You Know?

There are over one hundred billion brine flies around Great Salt Lake!

84

CHAPTER 7

UNIQUE ECOSYSTEMS

Deserts and rainforests are complete opposites, but they're both defined by how much water they receive. Although quite different, each is an interesting and important ecosystem.

An ecosystem is all the plants and animals, from microscopic to huge, that live in a place, as well as the physical environment itself—the soil, air, water, and even the sunlight. Everything interacts with each other. The plants need the soil and sunlight, the animals eat the plants, and the plants also depend on the animals.

DESERTS

When you think of deserts, you might think of blowing sand dunes, searing heat, and no water. That's partly right. Deserts in the United States have some sand dunes, but mostly they have soil or a gravel covering. It can be very hot, but freezing temperatures and snow occur too. The lack of water that defines a desert is unevenly distributed throughout the year.

The upper layer of desert soils doesn't have much **organic matter**. Below that top layer are clays, salts, and calcium deposits. Sometimes these layers are glued together by calcium carbonate—the same stuff that cement is made from. They form hardpans, called **caliche**, which are a barrier to rain. Usually a caliche layer is a ½ inch to 3 feet deep (1 centimeter to 1 meter), but it can be thicker in places.

Lack of water, hard soils with few nutrients, and searing heat make the desert a tough place to live. But plants and animals adapt in unusual ways. If you look closely, you'll see that many fascinating plants and animals live in dry places.

> ## WORDS TO KNOW
>
> **organic matter:** decaying plants and animals that give soil its nutrients.
>
> **caliche:** a hard soil layer of calcium carbonate, usually found in dry climates.

Desert Soil

Loose Soil (little Organic Matter)

3 ft.

Salts

Clay

6 ft.

Caliche

10 ft.

Bedrock

15 ft.

There are four deserts in the Southwest: the Great Basin, Mojave, Sonoran, and Chihuahuan Deserts. Arizona is the only state in America that contains all four deserts. The Great Basin Desert is the largest desert in the United States—larger than any single state other than Texas and Alaska. It is the northernmost and the highest in elevation of the four deserts, which also makes it the coldest. It is considered a "cold" desert because more than half of its precipitation comes from snow, and the temperatures are generally cold. Most of the plants are low shrubs, and there are hardly any trees or cacti. The most common plant is the big sagebrush.

The Mojave Desert is warmer, but still has hard freezes in the winter. It has a rainy winter season. Mostly low shrubs grow in the Mojave, and the only common tree is the Joshua Tree. The Mojave Desert contains Death Valley National Park, the lowest, hottest, driest place in the United States.

Did You Know?

Kelso Dune Field in the Mojave Desert has sand dunes as high as 650 feet (198 meters), and cover 45 square miles (117 square kilometers). Sand dunes make it hard for plants to take hold because the sands are always shifting. When people slide down the dunes slowly, it creates a low rumbling sound that can be heard and felt, called "singing sand."

JOSHUA TREE

It's prickly. It's spiky. It's NOT a cactus. It's the Joshua tree! The Joshua tree is a tree-like yucca that can grow as tall as 40 feet high (12 meters). Joshua trees don't have growth rings like other trees. Their trunk is made up of thousands of small fibers. But scientists believe Joshua trees can live hundreds and even thousands of years.

DON'T STEP ON THE UGLY DIRT!

If lack of water weren't enough for plants to deal with, they also have the problem of dry soil that's loose and always shifting, with few nutrients. That's where **biological soil crust** comes in. It's a mix of living organisms—mostly cyanobacteria (formerly called blue-green algae), along with lichens, bacteria, fungi, and mosses. It forms a web of fibers that binds the soil. So the loose, dry soil is held together, giving larger plants a chance to take root. Even when the organisms have died, the web still holds the soil together. Biological soil crust also fixes nitrogen, which most plants can't do. This means it takes nitrogen from the air and changes it into a form that plants can use. During the infrequent rains in the desert, the organisms in biological soil crust absorb 10 times their volume in water and then slowly release it.

So even though biological soil crust looks knobbly, dark gray, and ugly, it's really the most important part of the whole desert ecosystem. Without it, plants couldn't take root, and animals wouldn't have plants to eat.

WORDS TO KNOW

biological soil crust: a mix of living organisms that form a web of fibers that binds the soil.

succulents: plants with thick, fleshy leaves and stems that can store water.

Did You Know?

Even one footprint can affect biological soil crust for years. If you visit the Desert Southwest, don't step on the ugly dirt!

The Sonoran Desert is known for the giant saguaro cactus. It is the most diverse of the four deserts, with many types of cacti including prickly pear, organ pipe, and cholla. The Sonoran is also different from the other deserts because it has trees throughout. The hottest of the United States' deserts, it has mild winters without frost.

The Chihuahuan Desert is the southernmost desert in the United States. But it isn't the hottest because it's at a higher elevation than the Sonoran Desert. It still has frost in the winter.

The vegetation of the Chihuahuan includes low shrubs, cacti, and other succulents, such as yuccas.

SAGUARO CACTUS

The saguaro cactus is the symbol of the desert. It stands tall like a sentinel guarding the rest of the plants and animals. And indeed, the saguaro is the center of activity, home to woodpeckers, wood rats, purple martins, owls, lizards, and many other animals. Woodpeckers peck out a hole and the inside crusts over, forming a smooth hard surface. But woodpeckers like a new hole each year, so when they leave, other animals make their home in the abandoned holes. When the saguaro dies, these holes take much longer to **decompose** than other plant matter. They're called "Saguaro Boots." Like many desert plants, saguaros grow slowly. A saguaro that is 7 inches high (18 centimeters) is already 14 years old. And when the saguaro is about 12 feet high (3.5 meters) and 50 years old, it gets its first arm branching off. They can live up to 150 to 200 years, and the tallest known saguaro is 45 feet tall (almost 14 meters).

Saguaros adapt to the lack of water in a few different ways:

- Like other cacti, they have a thick, waxy outer layer that slows the evaporation of water. This layer is even thicker on the side facing the sun, to help the cactus from getting burned by the sun.

- They have far-spreading, shallow roots to quickly absorb any rain that falls, before it evaporates.

- Their outside layer is shaped like an accordion. When it rains, the saguaro can absorb lots of water because the folds in its outer layer can expand. A saguaro can gain up to a ton in weight from water in one rainstorm!

- They close their stomates during the day so they don't lose water. Stomates are very small holes in the leaves and stems of plants that take in and let out gases like oxygen and carbon dioxide—a bit like our breathing. These gases are necessary for the plant to make its own food, called **photosynthesis**. But stomates also lose water, so saguaros close them during the day when it's hot. At night saguaros open their stomates and take in carbon dioxide. They convert the carbon dioxide into another chemical that can be stored and used during the day.

WORDS TO KNOW

decompose: to rot or break down.

photosynthesis: the process a plant goes through to make its own food. The plant uses water and carbon dioxide in the presence of sunlight to make oxygen and sugar.

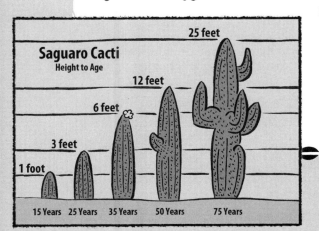

Saguaro Cacti
Height to Age

25 feet

12 feet

6 feet

3 feet

1 foot

15 Years   25 Years   35 Years   50 Years   75 Years

HOW OLD IS THAT PLANT?

Many desert plants grow very slowly and can live a long time.

WORDS TO KNOW

clone: an organism that is identical to those that came before it.

Bristlecone pine trees have polished surfaces that ring when you tap them. The oldest-known living organism in the world is a bristlecone pine called "Methuseleh," located in eastern California. Its exact location is kept a secret to protect it. Methuseleh is 4,838 years old. An even older tree—4,950 years old—lived nearby, but it was cut down in 1964. Why do bristlecones live so long? Scientists aren't sure, but the oldest ones seem to be at higher elevations, where there's thin soil and Arctic winds. It could be that there aren't many insects there. Or perhaps because the very hard wood they develop in the harsh conditions helps protect them from insects.

Creosote bushes can be found throughout all four deserts and other dry areas in the Southwest. They might take 10 years or more to grow a foot (30½ centimeters). When a creosote reaches about 6 feet in height (2 meters), things get interesting. The oldest branches die and the top stem splits into several pieces. That older stem dies, leaving a ring of stems that aren't connected. These stems are now "new" trees, but they came from the same original seed and the same genes, which means they're **clones** of each other. One ring of creosote bushes is 45 feet across (14 meters). Scientists have estimated this "King Clone" to be 11,700 years old!

ANIMALS IN THE DESERT

All organisms need water to live. When there's a lack of it, as there is in the desert, life adapts in many different and interesting ways. Some of the animals in the desert are unique to the desert. Others also live in other ecosystems, but have adapted their looks or behavior so they can live in the desert.

You'll find all kinds of animals in the desert—even fish and amphibians, although there may be fewer of them. Typical mammals include several smaller species, such as kangaroo rats, pocket mice, pack rats, ground squirrels, and rabbits. Larger mammals can include coyotes, badgers, foxes, bighorn sheep, and even wolves and mountain lions.

Deserts contain some interesting critters with unusual adaptations.

Spadefoot toads, like all amphibians in the desert, have it tough. Their young breathe water, and adults breathe partly through their skin, which needs to stay moist. To conserve water, spadefoot toads dig down 3 feet in the earth (1 meter) and become dormant for about 10 months of the year. Down in their burrow, they are protected from the heat and evaporation. They hardly breathe during this time. Spadefoot toads re-absorb stored water from their bladder into the rest of their body.

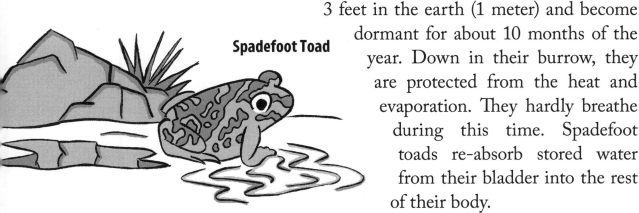

Spadefoot Toad

The summer rains wake up the toads, who then climb out. They reproduce, and while the newly hatched tadpoles swim in the pools of rain, the adults stuff themselves with insects.

Scorpions stay out of the heat of the day and hunt at night. Fine, sensory hairs that detect vibrations in the air or ground help them "see" their **prey**. A scorpion's hairs can detect tiny vibrations when an insect or spider walks across sand within about 8 inches of a scorpion (20 centimeters). The scorpion can determine exactly where the insect is and grab it with its front pincers and inject it with poison from the stinger on its tail.

Scorpion

WORDS TO KNOW

prey: an animal hunted by another animal.

predator: an animal that hunts another animal for food.

Pygmy Owl

Pygmy owls, like many desert animals, also hunt at night. They are only the size of a human fist, and love to nest in holes in the saguaro cactus. But they can eat twice their body weight in one meal. That would be like the average American man eating a single meal of 380 pounds (172 kilograms)!

Kangaroo Rat

Kangaroo rats, which are not really rats but are related to gophers, weigh less than half a pound—about as much as a granola bar (¼ kilogram). But because of their strong back legs, they can jump 9 feet at a time to escape **predators** (almost 3 meters). Kangaroo rats get water out of the seeds they eat. They also concentrate their urine so much that it's almost solid. This allows them to get by without drinking any water at all.

FROM DESERT TO RAINFOREST

Rainforests are the complete opposite of deserts. Much of the slopes of Hawaii's mountains and lowland areas are covered in tropical rainforests. They catch moisture from storms sweeping from west to east across the Pacific Ocean and receive 120 inches or more of rain each year (305 centimeters).

WORDS TO KNOW

endemic: a plant or animal that is native to only a certain area.

Rainforests are the most productive and diverse ecosystems in the world. Because Hawaii is more than 2,400 miles from the nearest continent (3,860 kilometers), it has an especially large number of species that are **endemic**, including fungi, mosses, snails, birds, and mammals. Most of the plants and animals on the islands are found nowhere else on Earth!

Humans have brought many new species of plants and animals to Hawaii in a very short time. Often, the native species have a hard time competing with these newcomers. There may not be predators, pests, or diseases that keep a new species in check, and it can take over. Scientists estimate that before humans, a new species arrived to the islands about every 30,000 years. Now a new species arrives about every 20 days.

Did You Know?

About 90 percent of Haleakala National Park's plants are found only in Hawaii, which places them at increased risk.

Gila monsters are large lizards that can grow up to a foot in length (30 centimeters). They have a short, thick tail that stores fat the lizard can use when it has to go without food or water. Most of the time gila monsters stay underground and inactive to conserve water and stay cool. Lizards and other small animals who live at White Sands National Monument have another problem. Their normally brown skin would stand out to hawks and other predators against the bright white of the sand dunes. They have slowly adapted to have white skin that blends in.

Gila Monster

MAKE YOUR OWN
AMAZING ABSORBING CACTUS

1 Fold the waxed paper along its width in a zigzag, accordion shape. The folds should be about 1 inch wide (2½ centimeters) and parallel to each other.

2 Place the roll of paper towels on a cookie sheet standing upright. Wrap the folded waxed paper around the roll of paper towels. Connect the ends of the waxed paper with paper clips at the top and bottom. The waxed paper should still have an accordion shape.

- sheet of waxed paper, 3 feet long (1 meter)
- roll of paper towels
- cookie sheet with rims
- 2 paper clips
- pitcher
- water

3 Slowly pour water over the top of the paper towels. Keep pouring until the entire roll is soaked. What happens to the size of the roll of paper towels? What about the waxed paper?

What's Happening

When the paper towels absorb the water, they take up more space, so the roll gets wider. It pushes against the wax paper. The waxed paper can easily expand because of the folds. The same thing happens in a saguaro cactus. It absorbs lots of water during rainstorms, and the accordion-folded shape of its outer layer allows it to expand in size.

MAKE YOUR OWN
TERRARIUM

1 Wash the soda bottles, remove the labels, and dry them. With help from an adult, cut the top off of one bottle, and cut the other bottle in half. Using two bottles allows you to make a taller terrarium.

2 Place pebbles in the bottom of the taller bottle to a depth of about 2 inches (5 centimeters). The pebbles will allow water to settle in the bottom so the soil doesn't get too muddy. If you have activated charcoal, place about ½ inch on top of the pebbles (1 centimeter). The activated charcoal helps to purify the water and keep the terrarium clean. If you have sphagnum moss, place a layer on top of the charcoal. The moss keeps the soil from settling into the charcoal. Finally, put at least 2 inches of potting soil on top (5 centimeters).

continues on next page . . .

SUPPLIES

- 2 clear, 2-liter soda bottles—one with the top still on
- scissors
- pebbles
- activated charcoal (optional), available at pet stores
- sphagnum moss (optional)
- potting soil
- seeds, or 2 to 3 small plants that like moisture, like small ferns
- pretty rocks
- water

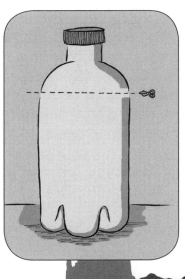

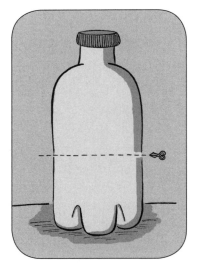

4 Gently pour water on the soil until it is damp. A small amount of water should settle in the pebbles. Take the top part of the bottle that you cut in half and slide it over the bottle containing the soil. The bottles should overlap about an inch (2½ centimeters). If you have difficulty sliding the pieces over each other, make small cuts in the top part. Make sure the bottle cap is on the top.

3 If you have seeds, plant the seeds to the depth noted on the seed package. If you have plants in pots, take the plants out of the pots and loosen the roots. Then dig a small hole in the soil and place the plant in the hole. Pat the soil around your plants or seeds. You can add pretty rocks or small sculptures as decoration.

5 Place your terrarium near a window, but not in direct sun. You can put the terrarium in the sun for an hour or so, but it will heat up too much if you leave it there for a long time. Every week, check your terrarium. The inside of the top should look misty, but not covered in water droplets.

6 Take off the top and feel the soil. Is it dry? If so, add some water. If the inside of the bottle is covered in beads of water or the soil is soaked, keep the top off for about an hour until the terrarium dries out a bit. If any plants are yellowed or a bit too large, gently trim them before putting the top back on. If a plant seems to be sickly or is very large, replace it with another plant.

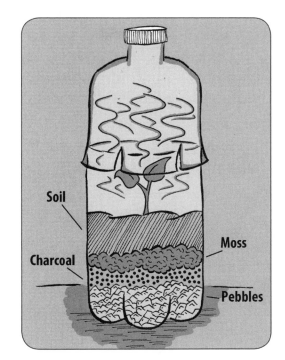

Soil

Moss

Charcoal

Pebbles

What's Happening?

A terrarium is a small garden that is grown inside a covered container. As the water is heated, it evaporates and becomes water vapor, which is a gas. Because the container is closed, the water vapor condenses onto the sides of the container. This condensation then "rains" onto the plants below, watering them. It's a continual closed-loop process that acts a little bit like a rainforest ecosystem.

CHAPTER 8

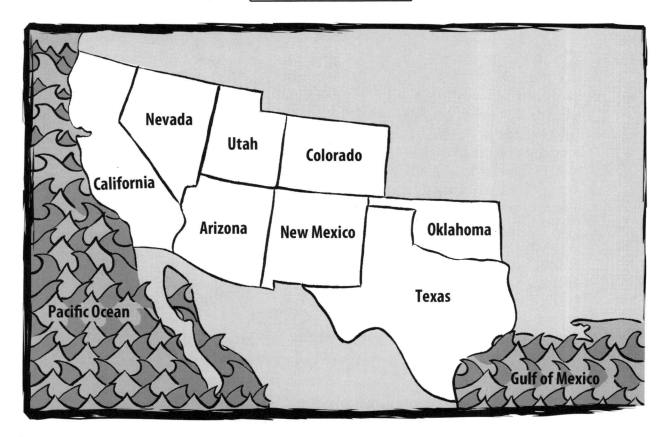

THE COAST

The Desert Southwest is the only region in the United States with coasts on either side. It touches both the Pacific Ocean and the Gulf of Mexico. A region that is known for its lack of water is surrounded by water! Each coast is quite different, with its own delights.

All oceans have currents. These are big movements of water over hundreds and thousands of miles. The current in the North Pacific moves in a clockwise direction. As the water heads east, it branches as it gets close to North America.

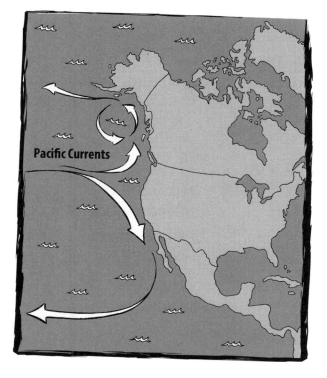

Pacific Currents

WORDS TO KNOW

upwelling: when colder, denser, nutrient-rich water rises to the ocean's surface because the surface water has been moved by wind.

phytoplankton: microscopic plants, usually single-celled, that drift on the current.

Some of the water flows south along the coast of Oregon and then California. This is called the California Current. Because the water in this current is coming from the north, it's colder than you might expect.

Upwelling makes the water even colder along the western coast of the United States. This happens when the wind pushes the surface water south and west—away from the land.

To replace this lost surface water, deeper water rises, or upwells, from down below.

Deeper water is colder water, and colder water has a lot more nutrients. These nutrients are used by **phytoplankton**, which are microscopic plants that fish love to eat. So it should be no surprise that the California coast is rich in fish and sea life.

The Gulf of Mexico is quite different. A gulf is a large area of ocean partially enclosed by land. Much of the Gulf of Mexico is relatively shallow, less than 66 feet deep (20 meters). This means that the water is much warmer than water in the Pacific Ocean at the same latitude.

99

In the Gulf, there is something called the Loop Current. Warm water flows north through the gap between Cuba and the Yucatan Peninsula in Mexico. It then loops around and exits back along Florida. Smaller loops of water sweep off the Loop Current, bringing warm water to the coast of Texas.

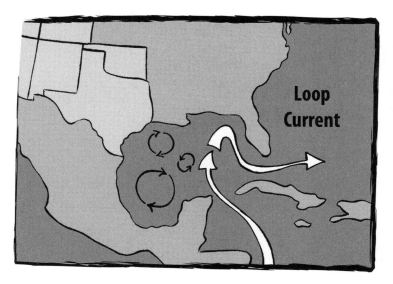

Loop Current

How big a difference in temperature is there?

In Freeport, Texas, the water temperature is 86 degrees Fahrenheit in August (30 degrees Celsius). On the west coast of Mexico at about the same latitude as Freeport, Tortugas only reaches 72 degrees Fahrenheit (22 degrees Celsius). That is a big difference if you're swimming! It also means that different types of plants and animals will live in the different areas.

HOW ACTIVE IS YOUR COAST?

The other major way that the two coasts differ is in how active they are tectonically. The coast along Texas is a **passive tectonic margin**. The transition here between oceanic and continental crust isn't active. Long ago, this transition was where rifting occurred, when a new ocean formed. But now, the boundary between ocean and continent has moved away from the rifting. Along passive margins, the land is called a coastal plain, and it's relatively flat.

WORDS TO KNOW

passive tectonic margin: where the transition between oceanic and continental crust isn't an active plate margin.

The weight of the sediments has pushed the crust downward along the Gulf so that some of the continental crust goes underwater at the coast. This land-to-sea transition, and continental-to-oceanic-crust transition, happens gradually because it's far from the edges of a tectonic plate.

This is a big difference from California, which is quite active! There, two plates are grinding past each other, causing earthquakes and volcanoes. The coast of California is filled with rocky shores and mountains that run right into the sea.

FISH!

The fisheries off both California and in the Gulf of Mexico are some of the most productive in the world. If you eat fish or seafood, you've probably eaten fish from these waters. Some of the fish caught are bonito, halibut, mackerel, red snapper, swordfish, tuna, squid, amberjack, tilefish, grouper, sardines, anchovies, and hake, as well as seafood such as lobster, shrimp, crabs, and oysters.

Many areas have had steep declines in the number of fish due to overfishing, pollution, and destruction of natural habitats. People have responded by banning nets from all Texas bays and limiting certain types of fish that can be caught. In many cases, the numbers of fish are increasing again.

Did You Know?

The male gafftopsail catfish and hardhead catfish incubate their eggs in their mouth. The male holds the fertilized eggs in its mouth for 30 or more days until they hatch and can survive without protection. The male can't eat during this time, but it gives the young a head start. That's one dedicated father!

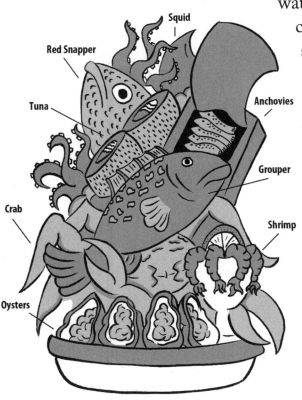

Squid
Red Snapper
Tuna
Anchovies
Crab
Grouper
Shrimp
Oysters

RED TIDE!

Red tide occurs where there's a higher-than-normal concentration of a kind of tiny algae. The algae in this type of tide produce a toxin that paralyzes fish. The algae occur naturally, but under certain conditions an **algal bloom** causes an unusually dense concentration. The water often looks reddish when this happens and smells like ammonia. Thousands of dead fish wash up on shore. Scientists aren't sure exactly why red tides occur, but it's probably due to some combination of higher temperatures, lack of wind, and rain. Red tide can occur both in the Gulf of Mexico and the Pacific Ocean.

WORDS TO KNOW

red tide: an algal bloom that produces toxins that can be harmful to organisms.

algal bloom: when algae multiply to huge numbers, sometimes changing the color of the ocean water.

kelp: large brown seaweeds that grow in shallow ocean depths. They form extensive forests that provide habitat for a wide variety of organisms.

barrier island: a long, narrow sandy island that runs parallel to the shore, built up by the action of waves.

CHANNEL ISLANDS NATIONAL PARK

These islands are isolated 100 miles from the mainland (160 kilometers), and unique plants and animals have evolved here. Located where two major ocean currents come together—warm from the south and cold from the north—makes for a place with an incredible variety of life. The Channel Islands contain over 2,000 species of marine life, as well as more endangered species than in any other park in the National Park Service. There are 145 species found nowhere else in the world!

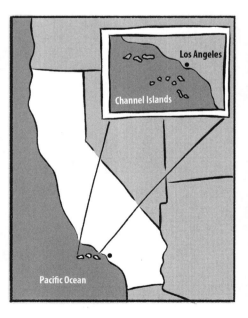

In this unique place, you can find forests of **kelp**. These large algae grow up to 2 feet each day (61 centimeters), and up to 100 feet deep (30 meters). Kelp forests are a haven for a huge variety of plants and animals, from sea urchins and cucumbers, to lobster, rockfish, rays, and eels. Tide pools, where the sea and land come together, hold starfish, anemones, crabs, and birds. And there are more blue whales here than anywhere else in the world.

PADRE ISLAND NATIONAL SEASHORE

Along the south Texas coast, Padre Island is the longest undeveloped **barrier island** in the world. The Gulf of Mexico lies to the east, and Laguna Madre to the west separates Padre Island from the mainland. Barrier islands stretch from Maine to Mexico, protecting the mainland from storms.

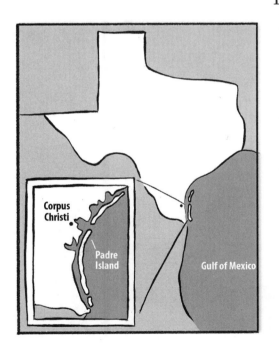

Corpus Christi

Padre Island

Gulf of Mexico

Padre Island formed as an underwater sand bar. Barrier islands have a natural cycle where they build up, then are stable, and then erode. The northern part of Padre Island is stable, but the southern part is eroding.

Over 380 species of birds, with 13 endangered or threatened, can be found on Padre Island. South Padre is in what's called the Central Flyway, which is the highway for birds migrating between North and South America. Birds stop here to rest, eat, and nest.

Five types of sea turtles nest here. Their numbers have declined because of loss of nesting areas and overfishing. Kemp's Ridley turtles, found mainly in the Gulf of Mexico, are the smallest and most endangered sea turtles in the world.

MAKE YOUR OWN
PURIFIED WATER

1 Fill the large bowl with warm water about 1 inch deep (2½ centimeters). Stir in a spoonful of salt until it is dissolved. Dip your finger into the salt water and taste it.

2 Place the small container in the middle of the large bowl. The top of the small container should be at least 1 inch below the rim of the large bowl (2½ centimeters). If it isn't, have an adult help you cut off the top.

3 Cover the bowl with the plastic wrap and put the rubber band around the rim to hold the wrap tight. Put several pennies on top of the plastic wrap above the plastic container.

SUPPLIES

- large bowl
- warm water
- spoon
- salt
- small plastic container such as a yogurt cup
- scissors
- clear plastic wrap
- large rubber band
- several pennies

4 Place the bowl on a shelf in the sun where it won't be disturbed. Wait a few days until the small container has water in it. Where did that water come from? Dip your finger in the water and taste it. Does it taste salty?

Salt Water

What's Happening?

When salt water warms up from the sun, some of the water evaporates and becomes water vapor. The salt does not evaporate. The water vapor then condenses into drops of water on the underside of the plastic wrap. The water droplets run down the plastic and into the small plastic container. This process occurs in the natural world too. Evaporation occurs from lakes, rivers, and oceans. Clouds form when the water vapor condenses into water droplets.

Some places that do not have enough freshwater and are near oceans use a process similar to this experiment to remove the salt from seawater. This is called **desalination**. There are a variety of ways to remove salt from seawater, but the main one is heating the water so that it evaporates, and then capturing the water vapor. Desalination requires a lot of energy to heat the water, so it is only used in areas without enough freshwater. Many areas of southern California have little water, but lots of people and agriculture. There are several desalination plants already built or in the process of being built along the coast.

Think About It!

Why do you think it takes so much energy to remove salt from water? What provides the energy for seawater to turn into the freshwater in our rivers and lakes?

MAKE YOUR OWN
WAVE TANK

1 Remove any labels from the bottle. Fill the bottle half full with water. Add a few drops of blue food coloring and one drop of green food coloring to the water. Slowly add the mineral oil.

2 Have an adult help you cut a piece of candle. Carve it into whatever shape you like. Drop the candle into the water. Screw on the lid and hold the bottle on its side. Tilt the bottle from side to side. Try tilting it fast and slow, as well as with big tilts and small tilts.

SUPPLIES

- 2-liter clear plastic bottle
- water
- blue and green food coloring
- ½ cup (118 milliliters) mineral oil or baby oil
- table knife
- piece of candle small enough to fit through the bottle opening

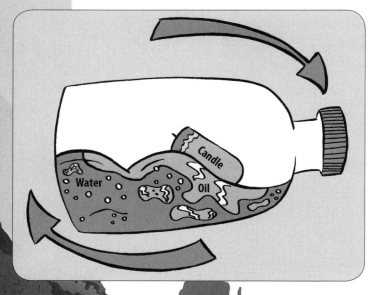

What's Happening?

The candle is less dense than the water or oil and floats like a boat on the water. Different things can make waves larger or smaller in the natural world. What makes your wave tank have bigger or smaller waves?

CHAPTER 9

NATURAL RESOURCES

Imagine if tomorrow there was no **crude oil** or natural gas. We couldn't drive our cars. Many of us wouldn't have electricity, heat, or air conditioning. The modern world depends on oil and gas, and much of what is used in the United States comes from the Desert Southwest.

WORDS TO KNOW

crude oil: petroleum oil as it comes out of the earth, before it is refined into other products.

107

WHAT'S IN A WORD?

What goes in a car to make it run? Gas, right? So is gas a liquid? Not really. We use the term "gas" as short for gasoline, which is a liquid that comes from crude oil. But the word gas usually means one of the three states of matter—solid, liquid, or gas. A gas isn't very dense because its particles are spread far apart from each other, and it expands to fill a container. Air is a gas. Natural gas is a special kind of gas made of carbon and hydrogen. Oil, also called **petroleum**, is a liquid. Sometimes it's so thick that it can almost be a solid. In Greek, *petra* means rock and *oleum* means oil, so petroleum mean rock oil.

WORDS TO KNOW

petroleum: a thick dark liquid that occurs naturally beneath the earth. It can be separated into many products including gasoline and other fuels.

plankton: tiny organisms floating in the ocean.

pores: small spaces in rocks or sediments that can hold fluids.

HOW OIL AND NATURAL GAS FORM

Oil and natural gas are organic, which means they come from living things. How could something once alive turn into gasoline for your car?

• Tiny, floating sea creatures called **plankton** die and fall to the ocean floor. They form a sludge of organic material at the bottom of the ocean. Over time, the organic sludge is covered by sediments like sand and mud.

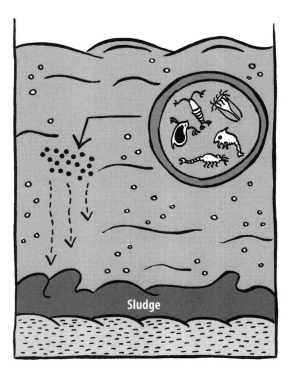

Sludge

• As the sludge is buried deeper and deeper by sediments, heat and pressure turn the material into oil or natural gas. At temperatures between 140 and 320 degrees Fahrenheit (60 and 160 degrees Celsius), oil forms. Between 300 and 570 degrees Fahrenheit (150 and 200 degrees Celsius), natural gas forms.

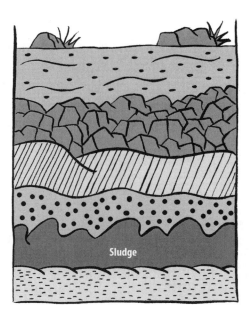

• Oil and natural gas are less dense than other materials, and will slowly rise through the rocks above it. For people to find oil or gas in large quantities, it has to accumulate somewhere. First, the oil and gas moves into rocks with tiny spaces called **pores**. These rocks soak up the oil like a sponge. The oil and gas also have to be trapped by other rocks that form a barrier. Otherwise, it would just keep rising to the surface. That might sound like a good thing because then people wouldn't have to drill, but oil that comes to the surface quickly decomposes. Oil was formed millions of years ago. If it had risen to the surface when it formed, it would be long gone by now.

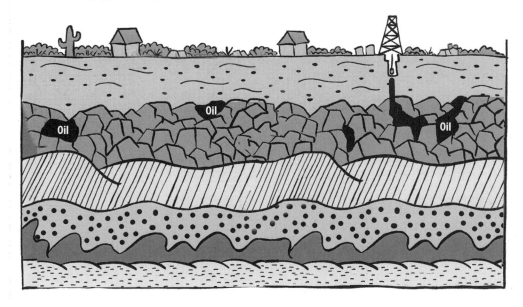

WORDS TO KNOW

wildcat well: a well in an area that isn't known to be an oil field.

seismic survey: a method used to explore for oil using sound waves traveling through the earth.

hydrocarbon: a chemical compound that contains hydrogen and carbon. Oil and natural gas are hydrocarbons.

fossil fuel: natural fuel that formed long ago from the remains of living organisms. Oil, natural gas, and coal are fossil fuels.

You might wonder how dry places like New Mexico, Oklahoma, and Texas could have buried sea creatures like plankton in their rocks. It's because millions of years ago, a shallow inland sea covered much of the central parts of the United States, including the Desert Southwest.

HOW WE GET OIL AND GAS

First, geologists have to find the oil and gas. That's not always easy, because it can be buried deep underground. People used to just guess where they thought oil and gas might be, and start digging. A well like that is called a "**wildcat well**."

Now geologists study the processes and structures in the earth to find oil and gas. Some types of rock are likely to contain oil and gas, while other types of rock never hold oil and gas. Geologists look for rocks that have lots of pores in them, that are capped by rocks that don't have pores. They take measurements and samples of the rocks underground. Sound waves are used to find the right kinds of rock underground because the waves travel through different rocks at different speeds. They move through liquids such as oil more slowly than through rocks. These **seismic surveys** measure sound waves as they come through the rocks underneath. Once a likely spot is found, drilling begins.

Did You Know?

Oil and gas are mostly made from hydrogen and carbon, so they are called **hydrocarbons**. They are also sometimes called **fossil fuels** because they formed long ago from plants and animals.

For deep wells, a drill pipe is sunk into the earth and a metal bit in its center is rotated very fast to tear away the rocks. When the oil is below the surface of the ocean, the drilling happens on the ocean floor. A huge platform is built to anchor the drill.

Oil Rig: Ocean Drill

Oil Rig: Land Drill

A GUSHER!

The modern oil industry began in Texas near the Gulf of Mexico. The area had bubbling gas that would catch fire. People tried drilling in the area, thinking there must be oil. But the first holes were dry. On January 10, 1901, at Spindletop Oil Field, things changed. A gusher, or blowout, gushed high in the sky—more than 100,000 barrels of oil per day! So much oil gushed out that it took nine days to control the well. It caused a rush to the area called the Texas Oil Boom. Gushers can be dangerous, and now companies have blowout preventers to control the flow of oil.

HOW WE USE OIL AND NATURAL GAS

Crude oil is a yellow-black liquid found underground. It smells. Crude oil can be very thick, like tar (heavy crude oil) or almost as thin as water (light crude oil). At a special factory called a refinery, oil is separated into different products such as gasoline, jet fuel, diesel, and heating oil. Refineries can be as large as several hundred football fields.

Natural gas is often found in the same places as oil. It is moved from the drilling site to where people need it using large pipelines. These pipelines can run for thousands of miles. Smaller pipelines connect to people's homes. In the summer, when not as much natural gas is used, it is often stored in large underground caverns.

Natural gas can be compressed and turned into a liquid, called propane. People use propane for backyard grills and camping stoves. Liquid natural gas takes up 270 times less space than when it's a gas. It's the same amount of energy squeezed into a much smaller space.

PRODUCTS FROM OIL AND GAS

Most oil and gas is burned to power our cars and make electricity. But it's also used for many other surprising materials:

- Aspirin
- Artificial limbs
- Car seats
- Bicycle helmets
- Basketballs
- Tennis balls
- Footballs
- Cell phones
- Tires
- Glycerin, used in toothpaste
- Fertilizer
- Lipstick
- Nail polish
- Balloons
- Bubble gum
- Crayons

OIL & GAS AND THE ENVIRONMENT

Oil and gas are important to our lives, but they can also affect the environment negatively. When people explore for oil and gas, they disturb the vegetation to build roads, drilling sites, and pipelines. The drilling can harm wildlife and produce air pollution. Water from drilling is polluted. Oil and gas can spill during drilling or transportation.

Working in the oil and gas industry can be dangerous for workers. Anytime huge pieces of machinery like drill rigs are used, workers can be hurt. Natural gas leaks can cause explosions and fires.

There are many laws and regulations that protect workers and the environment. These include having plans to prevent spills, and restoring the vegetation once drilling is finished. Some people think we have too many laws, and this forces us to rely on oil from other countries. Others think we don't have enough laws to protect the environment. What do you think? How would you find out more to decide?

113

MAKE YOUR OWN
OIL TRAP

- bathtub
- large plastic bowl, ideally transparent
- large piece of fabric with a tight weave
- large piece of fabric with a loose weave, such as burlap

1 Fill the bathtub with water. Place the bowl upside down on top of the water and slowly push it down into the water, keeping the bowl level. Can you see air inside the bowl? Slowly tilt the bowl until it's on its side. Does the air come out in bubbles?

2 Take the fabric with the tight weave and make a balloon shape with it, with the open side pointed down. Slowly push the fabric into the water with both hands so that air stays in the "balloon." Hold it underwater for a few minutes. Does the air stay inside the fabric balloon? Slowly lift up one side of the fabric to let any remaining air out. Repeat using the fabric with the loose weave.

What's Happening?

Once oil forms, it rises towards the surface of the earth. For people to find it later, it has to be trapped by rocks that form a barrier. The plastic bowl traps air like a rock that traps oil. Solid rocks can trap oil for millions of years until people come along and drill through it. Rocks that are like the fabric with a tight weave would eventually allow the oil to migrate upward. Rocks that are like the fabric with a loose weave let the oil pass right through to the earth's surface.

Oil and natural gas are often found around salt domes. Salt forms when an inland sea evaporates over time, leaving the salt behind. The salt can accumulate into thick deposits—hundreds, even thousands of feet thick! Later the salt is buried. When salt is under a lot of pressure, like it is when it's deep underground, it begins to move upward to where the pressure is lower. It's a bit like a lava lamp, or your bowl. The salt forms domes, and oil and natural gas can collect between the salt layer and solid rocks.

Did You Know?

Have you ever smelled natural gas? It smells like rotten eggs—yuck!! What you're smelling is a chemical called mercaptan. It's added on purpose by natural gas companies so that people will know if there's a leak. If natural gas is allowed to build up in a confined area, it can explode. So if you ever smell a rotten egg smell in a building, go outside and tell an adult.

accretion: the process of crust being added to a craton.

acequia: a community-owned and operated irrigation waterway.

adobe: brick made out of sun-dried clay and sometimes straw.

agriculture: growing plants and raising animals for food and other products.

algal bloom: when algae multiply to huge numbers, sometimes changing the color of the ocean water.

altitude: the height above the level of the sea.

aquifer: a large area of groundwater.

asthenosphere: the semi-molten middle layer of the earth that includes the lower mantle. Much of the asthenosphere flows slowly, like Silly Putty.

atmosphere: the air surrounding the earth.

barrier island: a long, narrow sandy island that runs parallel to the shore, built up by the action of waves.

basalt: a volcanic rock that is dark gray and fine-grained.

biological soil crust: a mix of living organisms that form a web of fibers that binds the soil.

brittle: describes a solid that breaks when put under pressure. A blade of grass will bend, but a dry twig is brittle and will break.

caldera: a bowl-like depression at the top of a volcano. It forms when the magma chamber underneath is emptied and collapses.

caliche: a hard soil layer of calcium carbonate, usually found in dry climates.

cinder cone: a small, steep-sided volcano, built by ash and small cinders.

cirque: a basin at the head of a glacial valley, which often contains a lake.

climate: average weather patterns in an area over many years.

clone: an organism that is identical to those that came before it.

Colorado Plateau: a large, roughly circular area of land, high in elevation.

Colorado River: the river that carved the Grand Canyon and flows at its bottom. The Colorado stretches 1,400 miles from the Rocky Mountains to the Gulf of Mexico (2,250 kilometers), and drops over 14,000 feet (4,267 meters).

continental: relating to the earth's continents. Continental crust is about 19 to 22 miles thick (30 to 35 kilometers).

convergent boundary: where two plates come together, forming mountains and volcanoes, and causing earthquakes.

core: the center layer of the earth, composed of the metals iron and nickel. The core has two parts—a solid inner core and a liquid outer core.

craton: the stable, central part of a continent.

crops: plants grown for food and other uses.

crude oil: petroleum oil as it comes out of the earth, before it is refined into other products.

crust: the thin, brittle outer layer of the earth. Together with the upper mantle, it forms the lithosphere.

current: a constantly moving mass of liquid.

dam: a barrier across a river to hold back and control the water.

decompose: to rot or break down.

dense: tightly packed.

desalination: the process of removing salt from seawater.

desert: an ecosystem that lacks water, receiving 10 inches or less of precipitation each year. Rain or snow is not evenly distributed throughout the year.

diurnal temperature difference: the difference in temperatures between the day and night. Deserts tend to have large diurnal temperature differences.

divergent boundary: where two plates are moving in opposite directions, sometimes called a rift zone. New crust forms from magma pushing through the crust here.

dormant: to be in a resting and inactive state.

earthquake: a sudden movement in the outer layer of the earth that releases stress built up from the motion of the plates.

ecosystem: a community of plants and animals living in the same area and relying on each other to survive.

elevation: a measurement of height above sea level.

endangered: when a species is in danger of going extinct, so that it no longer exists anywhere.

endemic: a plant or animal that is native to only a certain area.

erosion: wearing away of rock or soil by water and wind.

evaporation: the process where a liquid heats up and changes into a gas, such as water vapor.

evaporative cooler: a device that blows air over a moist surface. As the water evaporates, it cools the air. Also called a swamp cooler.

fault: a crack in the outer layer of the earth.

fossil fuel: natural fuel that formed long ago from the remains of living organisms. Oil, natural gas, and coal are fossil fuels.

geography: the study of the earth and its features, especially the shape of the land, and the effect of human activity on the earth.

geologist: a scientist who studies the earth and its movements.

geology: the scientific study of the history and physical nature of the earth.

glacier: a huge mass of ice and snow.

Great Basin: a large area covering most of Nevada, half of Utah, and bits of Idaho, Wyoming, Oregon, and California. All precipitation drains inward to the basin, with no rivers flowing to the ocean.

groundwater: water that is underground in the spaces and cracks between sediments and rocks.

habitat: a plant or animal's home.

hanging valley: a side valley that joins the main valley at a higher level, because it was formed by a smaller glacier that couldn't erode as deeply as the main glacier.

hoodoo: a geologic formation in the shape of a spire, usually with varying thickness.

hotspot: a small area where hot magma rises, usually in the middle of a plate.

hydrocarbon: a chemical compound that contains hydrogen and carbon. Oil and natural gas are hydrocarbons.

hydroelectric plant: a power plant that changes the energy from flowing water into electricity.

hydrosphere: the waters on the earth's surface, including oceans, rivers, lakes, and water vapor in the air.

igneous rock: rock that forms from cooling magma.

irrigate: to supply land with water using pipes and ditches, usually for crops.

kelp: large brown seaweeds that grow in shallow ocean depths. They form extensive forests that provide habitat for a wide variety of organisms.

latitude: the lines that run west and east on the globe parallel to the equator. Latitudes vary from zero degrees at the equator to 90 degrees at the North and South Poles.

lithosphere: the rigid outer layer of the earth that includes the crust and the upper mantle.

magma: partially melted rock below the surface of the earth.

mantle: the middle layer of the earth. The upper mantle, together with the crust, forms the lithosphere.

metamorphic rock: rock that has been transformed by heat or pressure or both into new rocks, while staying solid.

migrate: to move from one region to another when the seasons change.

molten: melted by heat to form a liquid.

monsoon: a wind system that brings heavy rains for one part of the year, and almost no rain the rest of the year.

moraine: an accumulation of gravel and sand deposited at the front of a glacier.

natural gas: a colorless, odorless gas that is used as a fuel.

Northern Hemisphere: the half of the earth north of the equator.

nutrients: substances that living things need to live and grow.

oceanic: in or from the ocean. Oceanic crust is about 3 miles thick (5 kilometers).

organic matter: decaying plants and animals that give soil its nutrients.

organism: any living thing.

Pangaea: a huge supercontinent that existed about 300 million years ago. It contained all the land on Earth.

passive tectonic margin: where the transition between oceanic and continental crust isn't an active plate margin.

petroleum: a thick dark liquid that occurs naturally beneath the earth. It can be separated into many products including gasoline and other fuels.

photosynthesis: the process a plant goes through to make its own food. The plant uses water and carbon dioxide in the presence of sunlight to make oxygen and sugar.

phytoplankton: microscopic plants, usually single-celled, that drift on the current.

plankton: tiny organisms floating in the ocean.

plateau: a relatively level, or flat area.

plate tectonics: the theory that describes how plates move across the earth and interact with each other to produce volcanoes, earthquakes, and mountains.

pores: small spaces in rocks or sediments that can hold fluids.

predator: an animal that hunts another animal for food.

prey: an animal hunted by another animal.

rain shadow: an area that is dry because it is on the side of a mountain away from the wind.

red tide: an algal bloom that produces toxins that can be harmful to organisms.

reef: a ridge of coral or rock close to the surface of a body of water.

GLOSSARY

Richter scale: a scale used to measure the strength of an earthquake. When the measurement increasing by 1, the strength of the earthquake increases by 10.

rifting: when the lithosphere splits apart.

sedimentary rock: rock formed from the compression of sediments, the remains of plants or animals, or from the evaporation of seawater.

sediment: loose rock particles such as sand or clay.

seismic survey: a method used to explore for oil using sound waves traveling through the earth.

seismic waves: waves of energy generated from earthquakes that travel through the earth.

seismograph: an instrument that measures vibrations under the ground.

shield volcano: a volcano formed from the flow of runny, non-explosive lava.

silica: a mineral existing in over one-quarter of the earth's crust.

species: a group of plants or animals that are closely related and look the same.

stratovolcano: a classic, cone-shaped volcano with alternating layers of runny lava flows and more explosive volcanic deposits.

subduction: when one plate slides underneath another plate.

succulents: plants with thick, fleshy leaves and stems that can store water.

tectonic: relating to the forces that produce movement and changes in the earth's crust.

transform boundary: where two plates slide against each other.

tributary: a stream or river that flows into a larger river.

upwelling: when colder, denser, nutrient-rich water rises to the ocean's surface because the surface water has been moved by wind.

U-shaped valley: a valley that has been carved by a glacier and has a shape like the letter "U," with steep sides and a flat floor.

vegetation: all the plant life in a particular area.

viscous: how easily a substance flows. Honey is very viscous, while water is not viscous.

volcanic dome: a volcano formed by thick lava oozing out. The lava is too thick to travel far and builds up into a dome.

volcano: a vent in the earth's surface through which magma, ash, and gases erupt.

watershed: the land area that drains into a river or stream.

wetlands: an area where the land is saturated with water. Wetlands are important habitats for fish, plants, and wildlife.

wildcat well: a well in an area that isn't known to be an oil field.

xeriscaping: landscaping with plants that need less water.

WEB SITES

- **www.eia.gov/kids/energy.cfm** U.S. Energy information Administration. Information about energy basics. Click on Energy Sources link for options on oil and natural gas, as well as other energy sources.

- **www.desertmuseum.org** Arizona-Sonora Desert Museum with information and activities related to the desert ecosystem.

- **mediaproductions.nmsu.edu/sw-horizon-bosque-del-ap.html** Video of the Bosque del Apache.

- **www.fws.gov/southwest/REFUGES/texas/aransas/whoopingcranes.html** U.S. Fish & Wildlife site with information about whooping cranes, and links for calls of the whooping cranes.

- **www.youtube.com/watch?v=pue6WAmcGtk** Video on red knot birds on Padre Island National Seashore.

- **www.earthquakecountry.info/roots/contents.html** Information about earthquakes in California and how to prepare for one.

- **www.maps.google.com** Satellite view of Desert Southwest, Pacific Ocean, and the Gulf of Mexico. Click on the Satellite tab and scroll to wherever you want to look. You can zoom in or out. Be sure to check out the Pacific Ocean and Alaska.

- **www.nps.gov/** National Park Service main web site. Click on links to find specific national parks and monuments.

- **tapestry.usgs.gov/features/23srnevada.html** Information on the Sierra Nevada, with links to the Basin and Range and California's Central Valley.

- **geoinfo.nmt.edu/tour/provinces/** Information on the Southern Rockies, Colorado Plateau, Basin and Range.

- **geomaps.wr.usgs.gov/parks/province/** U.S. Geological Survey with information on provinces. Click on areas in the map for more information on a province.

- **mineralsciences.si.edu/tdpmap/** World Interactive Map of Volcanoes, Earthquakes, Impact Craters, and Plate Tectonics, by Smithsonian, USGS, and US Naval Research Laboratory.

- **earthquake.usgs.gov/earthquakes/** Earthquakes in all states. Click on link on the left called "Info by State", then click on link "By State" to view information about a particular state. There are lots of other links with interesting information, including current earthquakes.

- **earthquake.usgs.gov/learn/kids/** U.S. Geological Survey (U.S.G.S.) Earthquakes for Kids site.

- **www.pbs.org/wnet/savageearth/** Volcanoes, earthquakes, tsunamis by PBS.

- **geoinfo.nmt.edu/faq/volcanoes/** Information on volcanoes in New Mexico.

INDEX

INDEX